Math LAB for Kids

FUN, HANDS-ON ACTIVITIES FOR LEARNING WITH
SHAPES, PUZZLES, AND GAMES

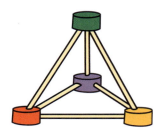

REBECCA RAPOPORT and **J.A. YODER**

Brimming with creative inspiration, how-to projects, and useful information to enrich your everyday life, Quarto Knows is a favorite destination for those pursuing their interests and passions. Visit our site and dig deeper with our books into your area of interest: Quarto Creates, Quarto Cooks, Quarto Homes, Quarto Lives, Quarto Drives, Quarto Explores, Quarto Gifts, or Quarto Kids.

© 2017 Quarto Publishing Group USA Inc.
Text © 2017 Rebecca Rapoport and J.A. Yoder

First published in the United States of America in 2017 by
Quarry Books, an imprint of The Quarto Group,
100 Cummings Center, Suite 265-D, Beverly, MA 01915, USA.
T (978) 282-9590 F (978) 283-2742
QuartoKnows.com

All rights reserved. No part of this book may be reproduced in any form without written permission of the copyright owners. All images in this book have been reproduced with the knowledge and prior consent of the artists concerned, and no responsibility is accepted by producer, publisher, or printer for any infringement of copyright or otherwise, arising from the contents of this publication. Every effort has been made to ensure that credits accurately comply with information supplied. We apologize for any inaccuracies that may have occurred and will resolve inaccurate or missing information in a subsequent reprinting of the book.

Quarry Books titles are also available at discount for retail, wholesale, promotional, and bulk purchase. For details, contact the Special Sales Manager by email at specialsales@quarto.com or by mail at The Quarto Group, Attn: Special Sales Manager, 100 Cummings Center, Suite 265-D, Beverly, MA 01915, USA.

10 9 8 7 6 5 4 3 2 1

ISBN: 978-1-63159-252-2

Library of Congress Cataloging-in-Publication Data available

Design and page layout: Laura Shaw Design, Inc.
Photography: Glenn Scott Photography
Illustration: J.A. Yoder & Rebecca Rapoport

Printed in China

The information in this book is for educational purposes only.

PUBLISHER'S NOTE Quarry Books would like to thank the staff and students at Birches School in Lincoln, Massachusetts, which graciously agreed to host the kids' photography for this book. We are especially grateful to Cecily Wardell, Director of Admission and Placement, who generously gave our authors, art director, and photographer access to their facilities and helped us coordinate their students' participation to minimize disruption.

FOR ALLANNA, ZACK, AND XANDER.

May you always find joy in math and everything else you do.

CONTENTS

Introduction 7
How to Use This Book 8

Geometry: Learn About Shapes 11

Prisms and pyramids and Platonic solids, oh my!

Lab 1: Prisms 12
Lab 2: Pyramids 14
Lab 3: Antiprisms 16
Lab 4: Platonic Solids 18
Lab 5: Perfect Circles 24
Lab 6: Try a Triangle 26
Lab 7: Exact Ellipses 28
Lab 8: Draw Giant Circles and Ellipses 30

Topology: Mind-Bending Shapes 35

Learn about squeezable, squishable shapes and surfaces

Lab 9: Compare and Classify Shapes 36
Lab 10: Möbius Strips 38
Lab 11: Möbius Surprise 42

Color Maps Like a Mathematician 45

Using the fewest number of colors possible, fill in a map so adjacent shapes are different

Lab 12: Map Coloring Basics 46
Lab 13: Efficient Map Coloring 50
Lab 14: Squiggle Maps 54

Stitching Curves 57

Learn to create curves using only straight lines

Lab 15: Drawing Parabolas 58
Lab 16: Stitching Stars 62
Lab 17: Creative Curves 64

Fantastic Fractals 67

A fractal is a shape that is similar to itself no matter how far you zoom in on one particular part

Lab 18: Draw a Sierpinski Triangle 68
Lab 19: Build a Sierpinski Triangle 70
Lab 20: Draw a Koch Snowflake 74
Lab 21: Draw a Square Fractal Snowflake 78
Lab 22: Explore the Koch Snowflake's Perimeter 80

Terrific Tangrams 83

Solve ancient Chinese puzzles by making different shapes from the same seven pieces

Lab 23: Tangram Basics 84
Lab 24: Teaser Tangrams 86
Lab 25: Tougher Tangrams 88

Toothpick Puzzles 91

Create and solve brainteasers using patterns of toothpicks

Lab 26: Starter Toothpick Puzzles 92
Lab 27: Toothpick Puzzles: The Next Level 94
Lab 28: Challenging Toothpick Puzzles 96

The Game of Nim 99

Learn the game of Nim and develop a strategy to win every time

Lab 29: Learn to Play Nim 100
Lab 30: Win Nim: The Copycat Strategy 104
Lab 31: Copycat Nim as Player 1 106
Lab 32: Win Nim: 1 + 2 = 3 Strategy 108

Graph Theory 111

Explore how points and edges are interconnected

Lab 33: Eulerian Circuits 112
Lab 34: Secrets of Eulerian Circuits Revealed 114
Lab 35: Bridges of Königsberg 116
Lab 36: The Euler Characteristic 118
Lab 37: A Proof About the Euler Characteristic 122

Pull-Outs 124
Hints and Solutions 131
Acknowledgments 142
About the Authors 142
Resources 142
Index 144

INTRODUCTION

WELCOME TO THE SECRET WORLD OF MATHEMATICIANS.

This is your introduction to the gorgeous, exciting, beautiful math that only professionals see. What's truly astounding is that it's *accessible*, even for kids ages six to ten. We think that if more kids had a chance to play with a wider world of math, there would be far more math enthusiasts in the world.

Most people think you learn math by climbing a sort of ladder: first addition, then subtraction, then multiplication, then fractions, and so on. In fact, math is much more like a tree. There are many different areas of math that require only a basic foundation. Plenty of this lovely and woefully ignored math doesn't require any previous knowledge. It's accessible to everyone, if they only knew it existed.

Readers of this book may ask, "How is this math?" Kids cut and tape and sew and color. They imagine walking over bridges, reproducing the same problem that spawned an entire field of mathematics. They draw enormous shapes in parking lots. It may not look like math because there are whole chapters with no pencils or memorization or calculators—but we assure you, the math you're about to encounter is much closer to what actual mathematicians do.

Mathematicians play. They come up with interesting questions and investigate possible solutions. This results in a lot of dead ends, but mathematicians know that failure provides a great chance to learn. In this book, you'll have a chance to think like a mathematician and experiment with a given idea to see what you can discover. That approach of just fiddling around with a problem and seeing what falls out is an extremely common and useful technique that mathematicians employ. If you take nothing else away from this book, learning to just try something—anything—and seeing what develops is a great skill for math, science, engineering, writing, and, well, life!

This is your opportunity, your gateway, into little-known worlds of math. Turn the page and explore for yourself.

HOW TO USE THIS BOOK

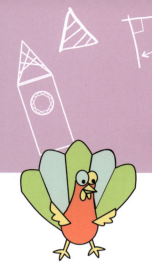

The chapters of this book can be worked in any order. Occasionally a chapter refers to a method learned in a different chapter, but there is always a work-around in case you haven't done the other chapter yet.

Within a chapter, we recommend working labs in the order given, as earlier labs often develop knowledge or tools you'll use in later labs within the same chapter.

All of the material in this book has been successfully play-tested by six- to ten-year-olds. We do assume elementary students will have a guide (parent/teacher/older sibling) to help them work through the labs. Much of the material should be interesting to middle school, high school, and adult students. There are cases where older kids will be able to try a more advanced technique and younger kids will do something easier, or may need a little help. For example, in the Fantastic Fractals chapter, older kids will use a ruler to find the middle of a shape, whereas younger kids can just "eyeball" and estimate the middle. Their results will be surprisingly close. Younger kids may need assistance with certain labs (tying knots, threading needles, cutting with scissors, etc.).

Each chapter introduction contains a **Think About It** question. The question is always related to the chapter's content and is meant to be played with *before* reading the rest of the chapter. This gives you the opportunity to experiment with the topic before we've introduced any formal concepts. Sometimes we come back to the Think About It problem within the chapter and answer it directly. Sometimes we don't. (In that case, if you're curious, check the **Hints and Solutions** section at the end of the book.) In general, we hope students will have time to experiment and not just race through each lab. Real math is so much more about curiosity and experimentation than most people realize.

Some chapters have **Try This!** problems that cover additional or more advanced material relating to the chapter. We provide hints for most of the Try This! problems either as the problem is stated or in the Hints and Solutions section at the end of the book.

Some chapters contain a **Math Meet**, a group activity meant to add a collaborative aspect to the learning process.

Each chapter just scratches the surface of a whole field of mathematics. If you're interested in more on any given topic, we've included some good sources

 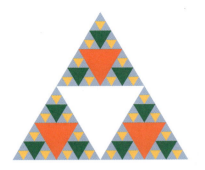 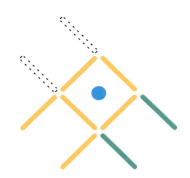

in the **Resources** page at the end of the book and also at **mathlabforkids.com** or **quartoknows.com/pages/math-lab**.

We tried to make the book completely self-contained so that you can work all the labs using simple household objects. For example, the graphs in the text of the Graph Theory chapter are large enough that you can trace them in the actual book. The maps in the Color Maps Like a Mathematician chapter are large enough that you can color them in. For a few of the labs, we have included pages at the end of the book that you can tear out and cut up or draw on. If you have access to a computer and printer, we also placed this content and much more on mathlabforkids.com. The website also contains larger versions than what's printed in the book for many of the exercises. You can download and print out as many copies as you like.

We'd love to hear from you about problems or successes you have with this book. Please get in touch with us via the contact information on our website.

We hope you enjoy this book as much as we enjoyed putting it together!

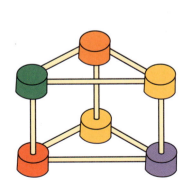  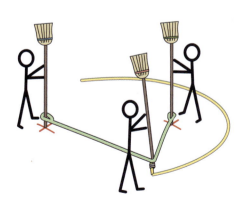

HOW TO USE THIS BOOK

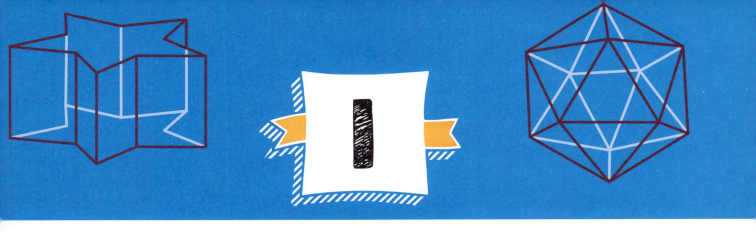

GEOMETRY
LEARN ABOUT SHAPES

Geometry is the study of shapes. There are a lot of different ways a shape can be. It can be flat (like a circle or a square) with two dimensions—length and width. It can be solid (like a block or a ball) with three dimensions—length, width, and height. A shape can be made from lines connected at corners (mathematicians call these edges and vertices; we'll learn more about those in chapter 9), or it can be made up of curves. A shape can have different numbers of edges and corners, or a different arrangement of curves from another shape. A shape can have different sizes.

In this chapter we'll make different types of shapes. Learning to recognize and make different kinds of shapes—to see what makes them similar and different—is a great way to start thinking about geometry and to see how we are surrounded by mathematical objects in our daily lives.

Imagine a triangle—it's a flat shape that you can draw on a piece of paper. Can you think of different ways you could build up a triangle into a solid object? What could those different shapes look like? How many can you think of?

LAB 1: PRISMS

Materials

- Toothpicks
- Gumdrops

Any flat shape can be made into a prism. In this lab, we'll use toothpicks and gumdrops to create three-dimensional triangular prisms. If you mess up a gumdrop, eat it to hide the evidence!

MAKE A TRIANGULAR PRISM

1. Make a triangle with three toothpicks and three gumdrops. To make it sturdy, push the toothpicks almost all the way through the gumdrops. Then make an identical triangle. These shapes will be strongest if you put the toothpicks into the gumdrops at the correct angle and don't reposition the toothpicks. With practice, you'll get better at putting the toothpicks in at the angle you want **(fig. 1)**.

2. Take one of the triangles and lay it flat. Stick a toothpick vertically (up and down) in each gumdrop **(fig. 2)**. What shape do you notice that the points of these three toothpicks make in the air?

3. Carefully position your second triangle on top of the three toothpicks from step 2 and connect the shapes into a *triangular prism* **(fig. 3)**.

4. A prism is an *oblique prism* if the top and bottom are not directly over each other when sitting flat on the bottom. Try making an oblique triangular prism **(fig. 4)**.

> **MATH FACT**
> ## What's a Prism?
>
> A *prism* is a solid shape in which the top and bottom are exactly the same, and all of the sides are rectangles.
>
>
>
> You can also make an *oblique* prism—the top and bottom are still the same, but the prism looks like it is leaning over. Now the sides are *parallelograms* (leaning rectangles).
>
>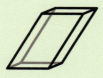

12 MATH LAB FOR KIDS

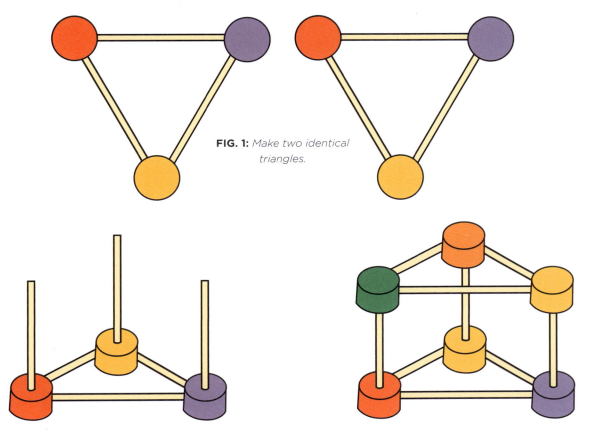

FIG. 1: *Make two identical triangles.*

FIG. 2: *Lay one of the triangles flat and stick a toothpick in each gumdrop.*

FIG. 3: *Place the second triangle on top to form a triangular prism.*

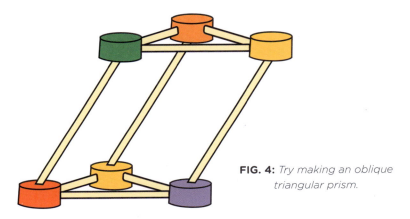

FIG. 4: *Try making an oblique triangular prism.*

TRY THIS!

Can you make prisms starting from a four-sided shape, a five-sided shape, and a star?

GEOMETRY: LEARN ABOUT SHAPES   13

LAB 2
PYRAMIDS

Materials

- Toothpicks
- Gumdrops
- Extra-long toothpicks, small baking skewers, or dry spaghetti or fettuccini noodles

MATH FACT
What's a Pyramid?

The Egyptian pyramids are one kind of pyramid, but there are many others. A *pyramid* is a solid shape, named after the shape of its base, which rises to a single point. All *faces* (sides) that aren't the base must be triangles, while the base can be any shape. If the *apex* (top point) of the pyramid is directly over the very center of the base so the pyramid looks like it is straight up without any lean, it is a *right pyramid*. If the pyramid is leaning, it is an *oblique pyramid*.

The three shapes above are all pyramids; the one on the right is an oblique pyramid.

Turn gumdrops and toothpicks into pyramids of all shapes and sizes!

MAKE A PYRAMID

1. Make a flat square using toothpicks and gumdrops **(fig. 1)**.

2. From each gumdrop, aim a toothpick upward at an angle so that they will all meet at a center point **(fig. 2)**.

3. Connect all the points with a single gumdrop. This is a "square pyramid," the same shape as the Egyptian pyramids **(fig. 3)**!

4. Now that you know how to make a pyramid, try making more with different base shapes, like a triangular pyramid or a pentagonal (five-sided base) pyramid **(fig. 4)**.

5. Using any base shape you want, make an oblique pyramid (it should look like it is leaning). The length of the sides going to the *apex* (top) of the pyramid will all be different, so don't use toothpicks; make the lengths you need by breaking the skewers or noodles **(fig. 5)**.

TRY THIS!

Can you make a pyramid starting from a star-shaped base? What other shapes can you turn into pyramids? Can you think of a shape that you cannot turn into a pyramid?

14 MATH LAB FOR KIDS

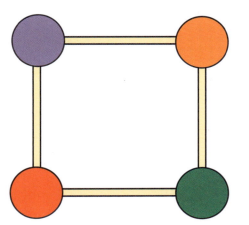

FIG. 1: *Make a flat square.*

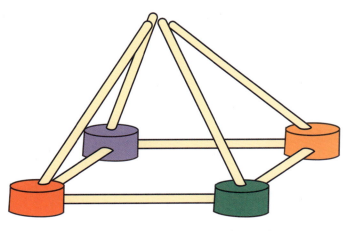

FIG. 2: *Aim a toothpick upward from each gumdrop so they meet in the center.*

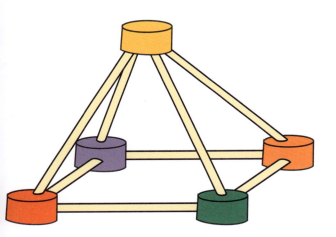

FIG. 3: *Connect all the toothpicks with a single gumdrop.*

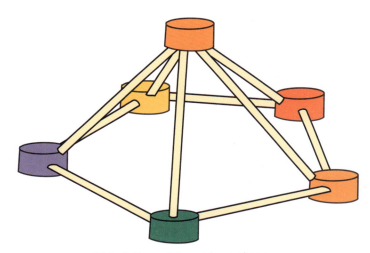

FIG. 4: *Try a different base shape.*

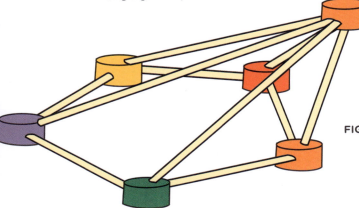

FIG. 5: *Using any base shape you want, make an oblique pyramid.*

GEOMETRY: LEARN ABOUT SHAPES

LAB 3: ANTIPRISMS

Materials

- Toothpicks
- Gumdrops

A PRISM has the same top and bottom shape, connected by rectangles or parallelograms. An ANTIPRISM also has the top and bottom shape the same, connected with triangles instead!

MAKE AN ANTIPRISM

1. Make two squares out of toothpicks and gumdrops **(fig. 1)**.

2. Hold the top square over the bottom one, then rotate it so that the corner of the top square juts out over the middle of the edge of the bottom square **(fig. 2)**.

3. We are going to make a triangle out of the corner of the top square and the edge of the bottom square. Connect this triangle with toothpicks **(fig. 3)**.

4. Moving around the shape, continue making triangles that connect the corner of one square to the edge above (or below) the other square **(fig. 4)**.

5. When you've completed the band of triangles to connect the two shapes, you've made an *antiprism*—a shape with an identical top and bottom, with all the side faces being triangles. It should look like a twisted prism **(fig. 5)**.

6. Try making a pentagonal antiprism and a triangular antiprism **(fig. 6)**. The triangular antiprism will be a challenge. Keep both—we're going to use them in Lab 4.

MATH FACT
What's an Antiprism?

The two shapes at the top and bottom of an *antiprism* are connected together with a band of triangles. Looking down, you'll notice that the top and bottom shapes don't line up but instead are twisted so that the point of the top shape is above the middle of the edge of the bottom.

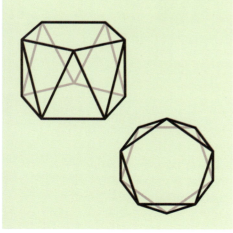

16 MATH LAB FOR KIDS

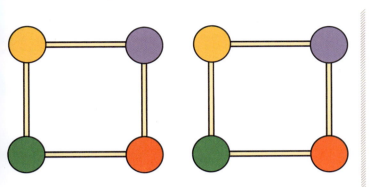

FIG. 1: *Make two squares.*

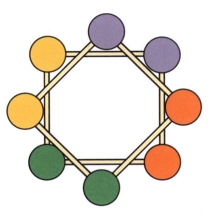

FIG. 2: *Hold the top square over the bottom one, then rotate it.*

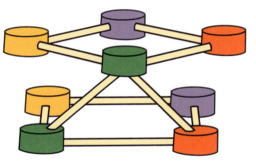

FIG. 3: *Make a triangle out of the corner of the top square and the edge of the bottom square, and then connect this triangle with toothpicks.*

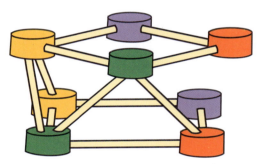

FIG. 4: *Continue making triangles that connect the corner of one square to the edge above (or below) the other square.*

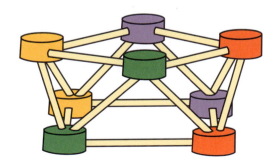

FIG. 5: *You've made an antiprism.*

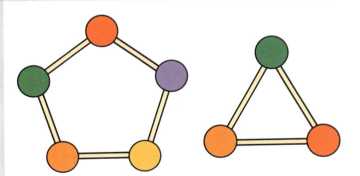

FIG. 6: *Get ready for Lab 4 by making a pentagonal antiprism (starting with a pentagon) and a triangular antiprism (starting with a triangle).*

GEOMETRY: LEARN ABOUT SHAPES

LAB 4: PLATONIC SOLIDS

Materials

- Toothpicks
- Gumdrops

MATH FACT
What's a Platonic Solid?

A *Platonic solid* is a solid shape that follows these rules:

- Each *face* (side) is exactly the same shape.
- Each *vertex* (corner) has exactly the same number of edges leading away from it.
- The length of every side is exactly the same.

There are only five Platonic solids: *tetrahedron, cube, octahedron, dodecahedron,* and *icosahedron*. Platonic solids are named after the Ancient Greek philosopher Plato, who described them around 350 BCE.

Tetrahedron   Cube   Octahedron

Dodecahedron   Icosahedron

Just about any shape can be made into a prism or pyramid, but there are only five Platonic solids.

ACTIVITY 1: MAKE A TETRAHEDRON

1. Make a triangle from toothpicks and gumdrops **(fig. 1)**.

2. Attach toothpicks to each gumdrop aimed upward toward a center point. Connect the toothpicks with a gumdrop **(fig. 2)**.

3. Verify that all the sides have the exact same shape. Count the number of toothpicks attached to each gumdrop. Each vertex (corner) should have the same number of toothpicks attached.

This is a *tetrahedron!* In addition to being a Platonic solid, it is an example of another type of shape from this chapter. What else could this shape be called?

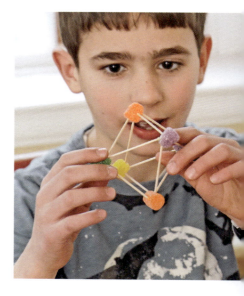

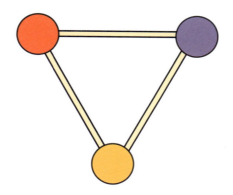

FIG. 1: *Make a triangle.*

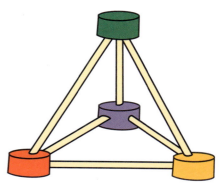

FIG. 2: *Connect a single gumdrop above the base.*

MATH LAB FOR KIDS

ACTIVITY 2: MAKE A CUBE

1. Make a square from toothpicks and gumdrops **(fig. 1)**.

2. At each gumdrop vertex, add another toothpick pointing straight up, and put a gumdrop on it **(fig. 2)**.

3. Connect the top gumdrops with toothpicks **(fig. 3)**.

This is a *cube!* In addition to being a Platonic solid, the cube is an example of another type of shape from this chapter. What else could this shape be called?

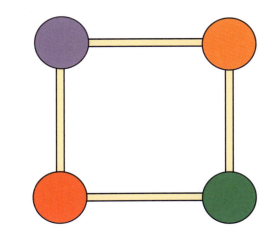

FIG. 1: *Make a square.*

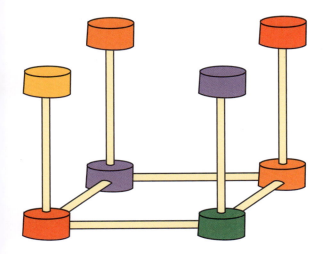

FIG. 2: *At each gumdrop vertex, add another toothpick pointing straight up, and put a gumdrop on it.*

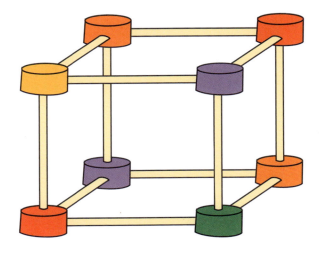

FIG. 3: *Connect the top gumdrops with toothpicks.*

GEOMETRY: LEARN ABOUT SHAPES

PLATONIC SOLIDS, *continued*

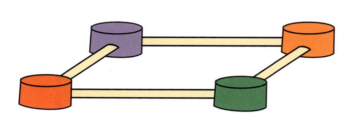

FIG. 1: *Make a square.*

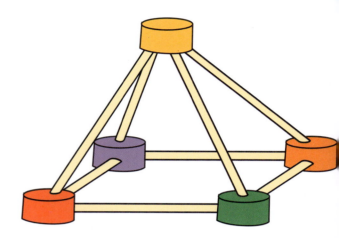

FIG. 2: *Make a square pyramid.*

ACTIVITY 3: MAKE AN OCTAHEDRON

1. Make a square from toothpicks and gumdrops **(fig. 1)**.

2. Make your square into a pyramid by attaching toothpicks pointing up at an angle so that all of the toothpicks come together at a single point. Connect all the toothpicks with a single gumdrop **(fig. 2)**!

3. Turn the pyramid upside down and make another pyramid pointing the other way **(fig. 3)**.

This is an *octahedron*! Like the tetrahedron, all of the sides are triangles. Can you find some ways in which the octahedron is different from the tetrahedron?

Compare the octahedron you built to the triangular antiprism that you built in Lab 3, step 6. What do you notice?

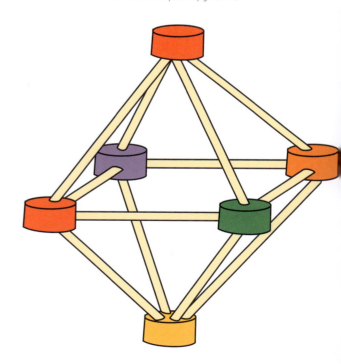

FIG. 3: *Turn the pyramid upside down and make another pyramid pointing the other way.*

ACTIVITY 4: *CHALLENGE!* MAKE A DODECAHEDRON

The *dodecahedron* has twelve sides, all of which are pentagons (five-sided shapes). It is the hardest Platonic solid to build, which makes it really fun! Don't expect to make a good-looking dodecahedron on your first try—practice makes perfect.

1. Make a pentagon from toothpicks and gumdrops. It should look like the template in fig. 1.

2. Attach a second pentagon to the first pentagon. A good way to start is to hold the pentagon from step 1 at an angle to the pentagon template **(fig. 1)**—that will show you where to attach the next toothpicks and gumdrops **(fig. 2)**.

3. Attach a third pentagon to what you built in step 2 **(fig. 3)**. Hold your shape so that the edges of your two shapes match two of the sides of the pentagon template. Use the template as a guide to add the next toothpicks and gumdrops.

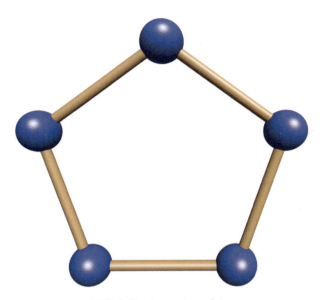

FIG. 1: *Pentagon template.*

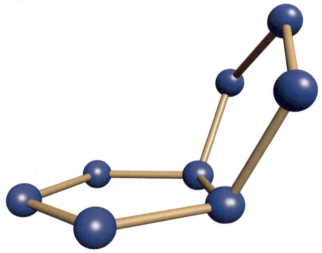

FIG. 2: *Attach a second pentagon to the first pentagon.*

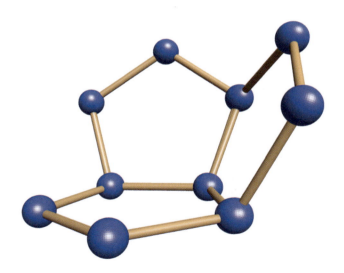

FIG. 3: *Attach a third pentagon.*

GEOMETRY: LEARN ABOUT SHAPES

PLATONIC SOLIDS, *continued*

MAKE A DODECAHEDRON, *continued*

4. You've added pentagons to two of the edges of your original pentagon. Keep going around the original pentagon, adding more pentagons as you did in step 3, until you have a bowl shape made from five pentagons **(fig. 4)**. This is the first half of the dodecahedron, but you're more than halfway done!

5. Add five toothpicks to the edge of the bowl at each pentagon's highest point so they angle in slightly **(fig. 5)**.

6. Make another pentagon with toothpicks and gumdrops. Attach it to the sticking-up toothpicks from your bowl **(fig. 6)**.

Congratulations on making a dodecahedron!

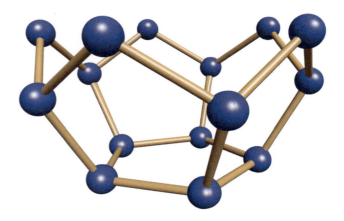

FIG. 4: *Keep going around the original pentagon, adding more pentagons as you did in step 3, until you have a bowl shape.*

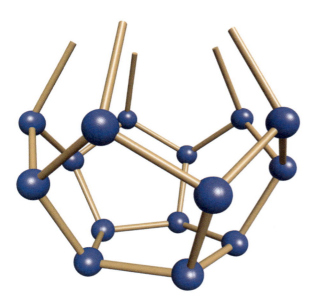

FIG. 5: *Add a toothpick to each of the bowl's five highest points.*

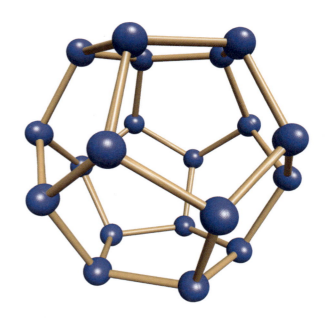

FIG. 6: *Connect a pentagon to the top of the bowl.*

ACTIVITY 5: *CHALLENGE!* MAKE AN ICOSAHEDRON

The final Platonic solid is the *icosahedron*. It has twenty sides, all of which are triangles. To make one, first make a pentagonal antiprism, like you did in step 6 of Lab 3 **(fig. 1)**. This will be the central ring of the icosahedron. Next, add a pyramid to the top of the ring **(fig. 2)**. Then turn the whole shape over and add another pyramid to the other side **(fig. 3)**.

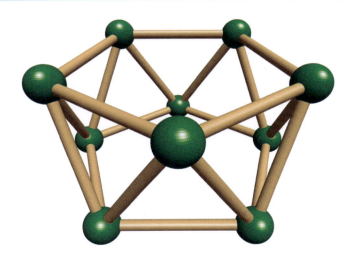

FIG. 1: *Make a pentagonal antiprism.*

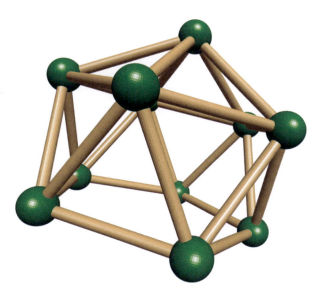

FIG. 2: *Add a pyramid to the top.*

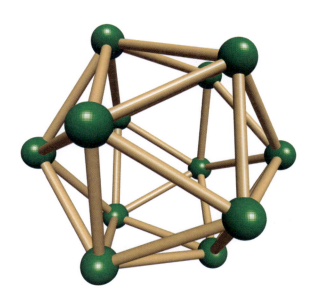

FIG. 3: *Turn the whole shape over and add another pyramid to the other side.*

GEOMETRY: LEARN ABOUT SHAPES

LAB 5: PERFECT CIRCLES

Materials

- ✔ Heavy string (about 10 inches [25 cm] long)
- ✔ Scissors (to cut string)
- ✔ Pencil or marker
- ✔ Paper
- ✔ Tape

It's difficult to draw perfect shapes freehand, so people have learned to use tools to help them. Using string, tape, and a pencil, we can draw a perfect circle!

DRAW A CIRCLE

1. Use the string to tie a loose knot around the pencil, so that the string can slip down and the pencil can freely rotate. As you draw, only the very tip of your pencil should be inside this loop **(fig. 1)**.

2. Mark the center of your piece of paper. Tape the free end of your string to that spot, with the edge of your tape touching it **(fig. 2)**.

3. Draw your circle by moving the pencil as far around as you can, always keeping the string taut. If your pencil is going off your paper, make the string shorter **(fig. 3)**.

4. Practice drawing circles of different sizes by changing the length of your string. Follow the tips on the next page until you can draw perfect circles every time! You can try drawing circles with different colored markers to make a whole rainbow of circles.

MATH FACT
What's a Circle?

A *circle* is a shape defined as all the points a particular distance (the *radius*) from a single point. In this activity, your string is the radius, and you move it everywhere you can around the center point to draw all the parts of the circle.

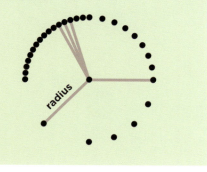

MATH LAB FOR KIDS

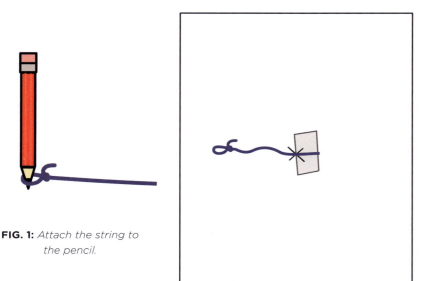

FIG. 1: *Attach the string to the pencil.*

FIG. 2: *Tape the free end of your string to the center of your paper.*

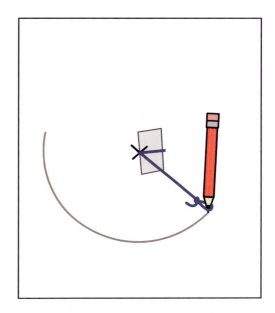

FIG. 3: *Draw a circle.*

TIPS FOR DRAWING AN ACCURATE CIRCLE

- If your string is slipping off your pencil, use a thicker string or twine. The tip of your pencil should rest in the small loop at the end of your string and drag the string along with it. If you have a thin thread, you can tape it to the end of your pencil slightly above the lead.
- Try to keep the pencil as straight up and down as you can. The more vertical your pencil is, the more accurate your circle will be.
- Make sure your tape at the center of your circle is really secure, and don't pull too hard on your string. You want the center point to stay the same the whole time you are drawing. It can help to hold down the tape with a finger.
- If you want to make more than one circle of the exact same size, mark your string at the center point. Then you can re-tape it in the same place for all the circles of that size you want to draw.
- Draw in small segments, and don't get frustrated. Every time you learn to draw something new, it takes practice!

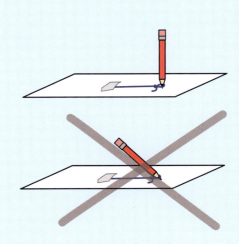

GEOMETRY: LEARN ABOUT SHAPES

LAB 6: TRY A TRIANGLE

Materials

- ✔ Paper
- ✔ Straightedge or ruler
- ✔ Pencil or marker for drawing
- ✔ Pen or marker to mark the string length
- ✔ String (about 10 inches [25 cm] long)
- ✔ Scissors (to cut string)
- ✔ Tape

MATH FACT
What's an Equilateral Triangle?

An *equilateral triangle* is a triangle where all of the sides are the same length.

Using string, a ruler, a pencil, and some tape, you can construct a perfect equilateral triangle.

DRAW A TRIANGLE

1. Draw one side of the triangle using the straightedge. Mark the ends of the line **(fig. 1)**.

2. Attach the string to the pencil like you did when you drew the circles in Lab 5 **(fig. 2)**. If your string is still attached from Lab 5, you're all set to go! If you know how to use a compass, you can use one instead of your string.

3. Mark your string with your pen so that the length between your mark and your pencil is the same as the length of the side of the triangle in step 1 **(fig. 3)**.

4. Tape the string to one end of your triangle's line, and draw an arc about where you think the third point of your triangle should go **(fig. 4)**.

5. Tape the string to the other end of your triangle's line, and draw another arc about where you think the third point of your triangle should go **(fig. 5)**.

6. The point where the two arcs *intersect* (cross) is the third point of your triangle! Use a straightedge to connect it to both marked ends of your first side to complete the triangle **(fig. 6)**.

26 MATH LAB FOR KIDS

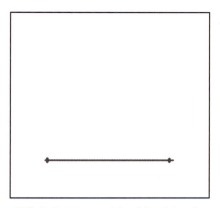

FIG. 1: *Draw one side of the triangle.*

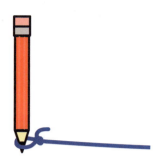

FIG. 2: *Attach the string to the pencil.*

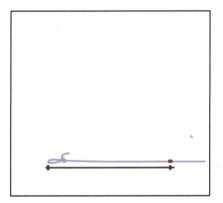

FIG. 3: *Mark the string with your pen.*

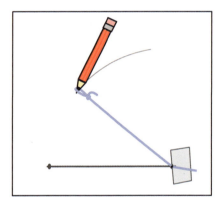

FIG. 4: *Tape the string to one end of the line, and draw an arc.*

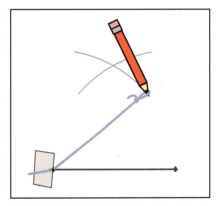

FIG. 5: *Tape the string to the other end of the line, and draw another arc.*

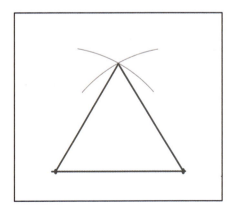

FIG. 6: *Connect the point where the two arcs intersect to both marked ends of your first side.*

GEOMETRY: LEARN ABOUT SHAPES

LAB 7: EXACT ELLIPSES

Materials

- Paper
- Pencil or marker
- String (about 10 inches [25 cm] long)
- Scissors (to cut string)
- Tape

MATH FACT
What's an Ellipse?

One way to define an *ellipse* is to start with two points (called *focus points*). The ellipse is made of all the points where the distance from the ellipse to the two focus points, added together, is exactly the same.

The legs from the two focus points are your string, and since your string isn't changing length as you draw the shape, you will end up with an ellipse.

A circle is a special kind of ellipse. If you make an ellipse but put the two focus points right on top of each other, you get a circle!

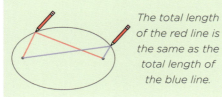

The total length of the red line is the same as the total length of the blue line.

We can also use string and pencil to draw special ovals called **ELLIPSES.** These are more challenging to draw than a circle, so be patient and try several times until you get the hang of it.

DRAW AN ELLIPSE

1. Mark two points a few inches or centimeters apart in the middle of your paper. Tape your string to the points so that the string has some slack **(fig. 1)**. For best results, arrange the tape exactly as shown.

2. To draw an ellipse, place your pencil against the string so that the string is taut, and lightly start drawing the shape **(fig. 2)**.

3. As you move around the ellipse, the string may twist. If the string twists around the pencil or the tape, that will make it shorter, and your ellipse won't be perfect. As needed, remove the pencil and reinsert it against the string to minimize twisting. Keep drawing in small segments until your ellipse is complete **(fig. 3)**.

4. Change the shape of the ellipse **(fig. 4)**. Ellipses come in lots of flavors, from very round to very oval. Try drawing ellipses starting with the focus points closer together or farther apart. Did the shape get rounder or flatter? What happens if the distance between the focus points is the same as the length of the string?

MATH LAB FOR KIDS

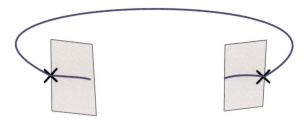

FIG. 1: *Mark two points a few inches apart. Tape your string to the points.*

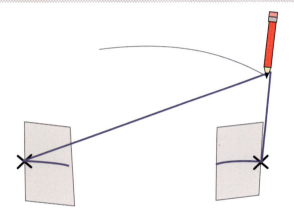

FIG. 2: *Grasp your pencil so the string is taut and lightly draw the ellipse.*

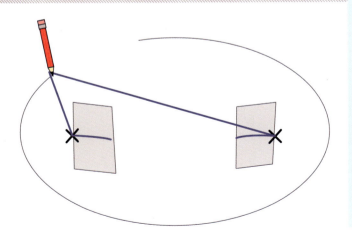

FIG. 3: *Keep drawing in small segments until your ellipse is complete.*

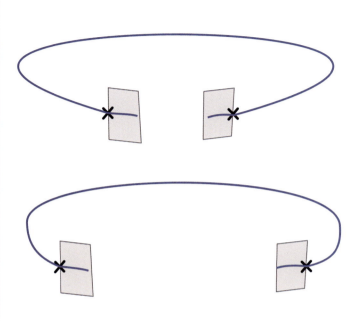

FIG. 4: *Change the shape of the ellipse by adjusting the distance between the focus points.*

TIPS FOR DRAWING AN ACCURATE ELLIPSE

- Draw the ellipse in short pieces. Insert your pencil, use a light back-and-forth motion, then remove your pencil. Keep redoing this process with a new section of the ellipse until you've drawn the entire shape.
- Make sure the tape at the focus points is secure.
- If you're having trouble with your string slipping off of your pencil, use a rubber band to make a barrier to keep it in place, as close to the point of the pencil as you can.
- Keep your pencil straight up and down, not leaning.

GEOMETRY: LEARN ABOUT SHAPES   29

LAB 8: DRAW GIANT CIRCLES AND ELLIPSES

Materials

✔ Sidewalk chalk

✔ Three broomsticks

✔ Packing tape, duct tape, or lots of masking tape

✔ Sturdy string, twine, or rope, at least 3 feet (92 cm) long for a circle, or 5 feet (1.5 m) for an ellipse

✔ Scissors (to cut the string)

✔ Two people for a giant circle, three for a giant ellipse

Sometimes bigger is better! We can use the same string techniques (and some friends) to draw giant circles and ellipses outside using sidewalk chalk. Make sure you have permission to draw on the sidewalk or driveway before you begin!

ACTIVITY 1: MAKE A GIANT CIRCLE

1. Make a giant "pencil" by attaching the chalk to the side of one end of a broomstick using tape. Make sure it is sturdy! You don't want your chalk to fall off **(fig. 1)**.

2. Tie a loop at each end of your string. The loops should be large enough so that you can slip the broomsticks and your giant "pencil" inside easily **(fig. 2)**.

3. Mark the center of your giant circle with chalk. (X marks the spot!) Have one person stand at the center with a broomstick and slip one loop of your string over the broomstick **(fig. 3)**. That person's job is to keep the broomstick always right over the center mark, and to stay out of the way of the string!

4. The second person should slip the other loop over the end of the giant "pencil." Then, keeping the string taut at all times, he or she will walk around the person in the middle, drawing at the same time **(fig. 4)**. He or she must keep the string taut without pulling the center off the mark, while avoiding being tangled up in the string.

MATH LAB FOR KIDS

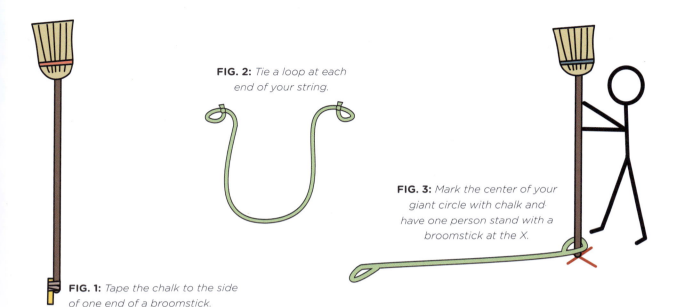

FIG. 1: *Tape the chalk to the side of one end of a broomstick.*

FIG. 2: *Tie a loop at each end of your string.*

FIG. 3: *Mark the center of your giant circle with chalk and have one person stand with a broomstick at the X.*

FIG. 4: *Keeping the string taut, walk in a circle, drawing as you go.*

TIPS FOR DRAWING ACCURATE GIANT SHAPES

- The "center" person needs to hold tightly to his or her broomstick so that the center doesn't slip.
- The "drawing" person needs to be careful not to pull too hard on the string; sharp tugs will pull the center away. Work together as a team!
- Try to keep the broomsticks *vertical*—straight up and down, with no lean.
- If the center broomstick slips, stop drawing until it is back in place. That's why we marked the center point(s)—so we can put it back where it belongs!
- This is truly a team effort, and it is difficult to draw an accurate giant circle or ellipse. Give everyone on your drawing team a high five when you manage to draw one.

GEOMETRY: LEARN ABOUT SHAPES

DRAW GIANT CIRCLES AND ELLIPSES, *continued*

ACTIVITY 2: *CHALLENGE!* MAKE A GIANT ELLIPSE

This one is hard! Can you (and two friends) do it?

1. Mark two points on the ground that are closer together than the length of your string.

2. Slip the ends of the looped string over the plain broomsticks (not your giant pencil). You'll need two people to hold them—one for each broomstick. Put the broomsticks on top of the marks you drew in step 1 **(fig. 1)**.

3. The third person will draw the ellipse with the giant pencil. This is best done in several short sections instead of one continuous curve; everyone is going to be dodging string and broomsticks! Just do one little piece of the ellipse at a time **(fig. 2)**.

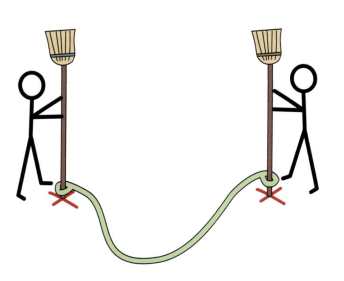

FIG. 1: *Slip the ends of the looped string over the broomsticks and put them over the marks you drew in step 1.*

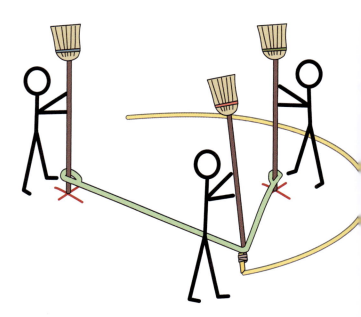

FIG. 2: *Draw the ellipse with the giant pencil, one section at a time.*

MATH LAB FOR KIDS

2

TOPOLOGY
MIND-BENDING SHAPES

Topology is one of many ways to study shapes. In topology, you can deform, or change, a shape in certain ways—by stretching, bulging, or squeezing—without turning it into a different shape. However, the rules of topology say you can't glue a shape to itself or poke a hole in it, because if you do that, you've created a new shape. Topologists study these changeable shapes to explore what other properties of a shape are still important.

Topology is also the study of spaces and how they're connected. For example, the space occupied by your house is made up of smaller spaces (rooms) connected in a particular way (doors, hallways, and so on). Topologists study knots, mazes, and lots of other interesting shapes. Their findings have helped make advances in many fields, including robotics (navigation), computer science (computer networks), biology (gene regulation), and chemistry (molecular shapes).

Compare a ball and a book. In what ways are their shapes different? In what ways are they the same?

LAB 9: COMPARE AND CLASSIFY SHAPES

Materials

- ✔ Scissors
- ✔ Large rubber balloon
- ✔ Marker
- ✔ A plastic sandwich bag loosely filled with clay or playdoh and then closed
- ✔ Paper and pencil
- ✔ A ball, a small bowl or box, a mug with a handle, and a bagel (or any doughnut-shaped item with a hole in the middle)

MATH MEET
Name That Shape

Topologists *classify* shapes by putting them into categories. This is a fun contest for you and some friends. In five minutes:

- Who can classify the most shapes according to their number of holes?
- Who can find at least one object with zero, one, two, three, four, and five holes?
- Who can find the object with the most holes?
- Can you find a shape that your friends won't be able to classify? Bring your confusing shapes together and see if you can figure out how many holes they have!

In topology, you can stretch, squeeze, or twist a shape without changing what kind of shape it is. We'll explore how shapes are allowed to change in topology by transforming one shape into some others.

ACTIVITY 1: TRANSFORMING A CIRCLE

1. Cut the balloon in half lengthwise so that you have a sheet of rubber.

2. With the marker, draw a circle on the rubber sheet **(fig. 1)**.

3. Try to transform the circle into a square by pulling on the edges of the rubber sheet. You might need more than two hands to do it **(fig. 2)**!

4. Can you turn the circle into a triangle by pulling on the sheet? What other shapes can you transform the circle into? Because you didn't poke a hole, cut the sheet, tape parts of it together, or draw another line, topologists consider all of these the same shape.

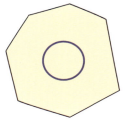

FIG. 1: *Draw a circle onto the rubber sheet.*

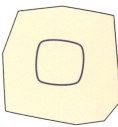

FIG. 2: *Pull on the edges of the rubber sheet to transform the circle into a square and other shapes.*

36   MATH LAB FOR KIDS

ACTIVITY 2: TRANSFORMING WITH CLAY

Next we'll use the bag of clay. Without poking a hole in the bag, or taping parts of it together, which of the shapes below can you make the bag look like?

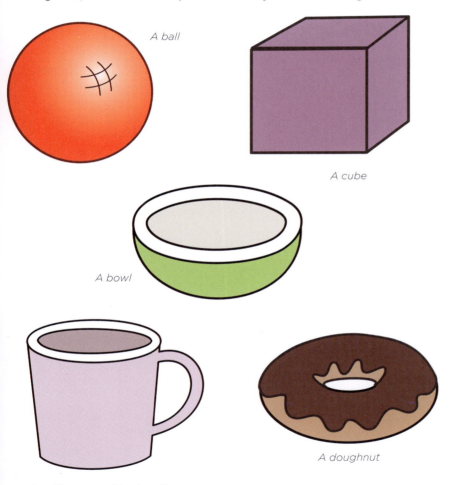

A ball

A cube

A bowl

A coffee mug with a handle

A doughnut

Which shapes could you make? To a topologist, those are the "same" shape, because they each have zero holes. How many holes are in the doughnut and the coffee mug?

Scavenger Hunt

One way topologists classify shapes is by how many holes they have. A ball has zero holes. A doughnut has one hole. A pot with a handle on each side has two holes.

Divide your paper into four sections labeled "zero," "one," "two," and "lots." Look around your house or classroom to find objects. Figure out how many holes each object has and write them on your paper.

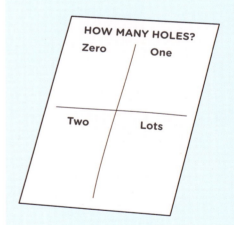

TOPOLOGY: MIND-BENDING SHAPES   37

LAB 10: MÖBIUS STRIPS

Materials

- Four strips of white paper about 2 inches (5 cm) wide and 22 to 24 inches (56 to 61 cm) long. *You can make long strips by taping together two strips cut from one 8.5 x 11-inch (21.6 x 27.9 cm) sheet, but make sure the tape covers the whole width of the strip.*
- Tape
- Markers in at least two different colors
- Scissors

MATH FACT

What's a Möbius Strip?

A Möbius strip is a surface that has only one side and only one edge. When you draw a line down the center of a Möbius strip, you'll notice that the line goes on what used to be both sides of the original paper before you twisted it, so the line you drew is twice the length of your strip of paper!

Turn a piece of paper that has two sides and four edges into a shape that has only one side and one edge.

ACTIVITY 1: MAKE A CROWN AND A MÖBIUS STRIP

1. Before you begin, examine a strip of paper. It has two sides (front and back), and four edges (top, bottom, left, and right).

2. Make a crown by taking one strip of paper and taping the ends together, making sure there are no twists. Tape across the whole width of the strip. See if it fits smoothly on your head, like a crown **(fig. 1)**.

3. To make a Möbius strip, bring the ends of another strip of paper together (as if you're going to make another crown), then use one hand to twist one end of the strip upside down. Tape the ends together across the whole width of the strip **(fig. 2)**.

4. On your crown, carefully use a marker to draw a line down the center all the way around until the line meets up with itself. Using a different color, draw another line all the way around the inside of the crown. (You can gently turn the crown inside out to make it easier.) Notice that the crown has two "sides"—an inside and an outside—that are now marked with two different colors **(fig. 3)**.

5. Count how many edges the crown has. Does it have the same number of edges as the strip of paper you made it out of? No—a strip of paper has four edges, but the crown has only two.

6. On your Möbius strip, carefully draw a line down the center until the line meets up with itself **(fig. 4)**.

7. What do you notice about your Möbius strip? How many sides does it have? Count its edges. It should have one side and one edge—that's what makes it a Möbius strip. Can you think of any other shape that has only one edge?

MATH LAB FOR KIDS

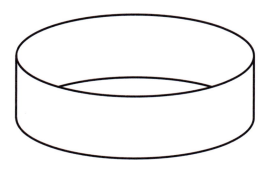

FIG. 1: *Make a crown by taping the ends of a strip of paper together.*

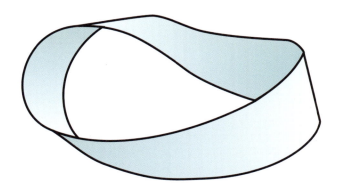

FIG. 2: *Make a Möbius strip by bringing the ends of a strip of paper together, twisting one end of the strip upside down, then taping the two ends together.*

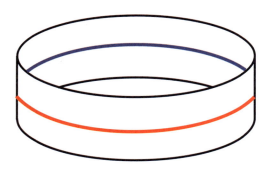

FIG. 3: *Draw a line around the center of the outside of the crown. Use a second color to draw a line around the inside.*

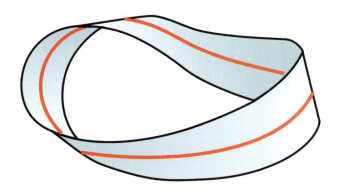

FIG. 4: *Draw a line around the center of the Möbius strip.*

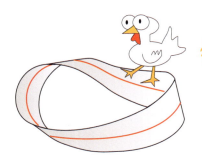

MATH JOKE

Q: Why did the chicken cross the Möbius strip?

A: To get to the same side!

TOPOLOGY: MIND-BENDING SHAPES

MÖBIUS STRIPS, *continued*

ACTIVITY 2: CUT THE MÖBIUS STRIP AND CROWN

1. Take your crown from Activity 1 and carefully cut down the center of the strip using the line you drew as a guide **(fig. 5)**. How many pieces did you end up with? Was it what you expected?

2. Do the same with your Möbius strip **(fig. 6)**. What happened? Was it what you expected? Is there a Möbius strip in the resulting shape(s)? How can you tell, using a marker?

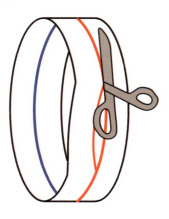

FIG. 5: *Take your crown and carefully cut down the center of the strip.*

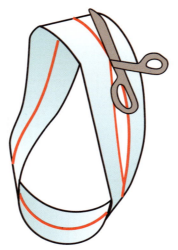

FIG. 6: *Do the same with your Möbius strip and see what happens.*

TRY THIS!

We made a Möbius strip by adding one half-twist to our paper before we taped it together. Try making rings with two half-twists, three half-twists, and four half-twists (you may need a longer strip of paper for these shapes). Using a marker, see if any of these shapes are more like our original crown or a Möbius strip. Do you see a pattern? Try cutting these strips down the middle. What happens?

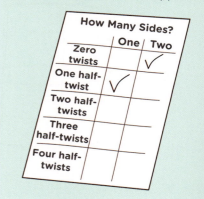

What's Going On?

When you cut a Möbius strip in half, you end up with a single long band that has two full twists. This band has two sides and two edges. The line you cut became the second edge. It's no longer a Möbius strip!

Counting the twists in the band can be confusing. The original Möbius strip had a half twist in it. After you cut it, each half of the original strip contributes half a twist to the final band, which accounts for one of the twists. In addition, the band is looped once around itself. When you unwind it to see the full band, that's where the second twist comes from!

Notice how the cut strip loops around itself. When you open up the band, that puts an extra twist in your final shape!

Materials

- Two strips of white paper about 2 inches (5 cm) wide and 22 to 24 inches (56 to 61 cm) long
  You can make these by taping two strips cut from an 8.5 x 11-inch (21.6 x 27.9 cm) sheet together, but make sure the tape covers the whole width of the strip.
- Tape
- Markers in at least two different colors
- Scissors

ACTIVITY 3: CUT A MÖBIUS STRIP AND CROWN INTO THIRDS

1. Make a new paper crown and a new Möbius strip with the strips of paper.

2. Carefully draw a line around the crown again, this time about a third of the way from the edge. (Don't worry if it's not exactly a third.) Using a different color, draw another line about a third of the way from the other edge **(fig. 1)**. Do the same thing with your Möbius strip **(fig. 2)**. What is different between the lines you drew on the crown and on the Möbius strip?

3. Cut the paper crown along the lines that you drew **(fig. 3)**. What shapes do you end up with?

4. Before you cut your Möbius strip into thirds, try to guess what shape or shapes you'll end up with—how many pieces, with how many twists? Once you've made your guess, cut the Möbius strip using your lines as a guide **(fig. 4)**. What do you end up with? Is it what you expected? Use a marker to figure out if any of the shapes are Möbius strips.

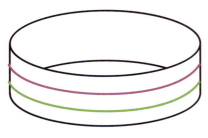

FIG. 1: *Carefully draw a line around the crown about a third of the way from each edge.*

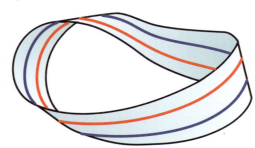

FIG. 2: *Do the same thing with your Möbius strip.*

FIG. 3: *Cut the paper crown along the lines that you drew.*

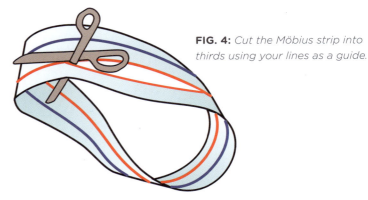

FIG. 4: *Cut the Möbius strip into thirds using your lines as a guide.*

TOPOLOGY: MIND-BENDING SHAPES

LAB 11
MÖBIUS SURPRISE

Materials

- ✔ Paper (8.5 × 11 inches [21.6 × 27.9 cm])
- ✔ Markers in two different colors
- ✔ Tape
- ✔ Scissors

Martin Gardner, a mathematician famous for introducing fun mathematical challenges to the public, invented an entertaining surprise using the concepts we just learned. Try it for yourself!

TRY THE MÖBIUS SURPRISE

1. Draw a thick plus sign on a piece of white paper. Cut out the shape. Draw a single solid line across the short arm of the plus sign. Turn the shape over, and draw the same line on the back. Draw two dotted vertical lines dividing the long arm of the plus sign into equal widths. Turn the shape over and repeat these lines on the back of the paper **(fig. 1)**.

2. Take the two horizontal arms, with the single solid line on them, and tape the edges together without any twists to form a ring. Make sure the tape goes all the way across the joint so that it won't fall apart later **(fig. 2)**.

3. Take the remaining two arms and tape them into a Möbius strip opposite your original ring **(fig. 3)**.

4. Before you cut along your lines, try to guess what the final shape will be **(fig. 5)**. Will it be a giant ring? Several interlocked rings? Some other shape?

5. The order that you cut the lines is important. First, cut along the dotted lines (they should be on the twisted ring of the surprise). Next, cut along the solid line **(fig. 4)**. What do you end up with?

TRY THIS!

The Möbius surprise is made by connecting a ring and a Möbius strip and cutting them. Try inventing other combinations of shapes and twists, cutting them, and seeing what you end up with. Can you invent a surprise shape named after you?

42   MATH LAB FOR KIDS

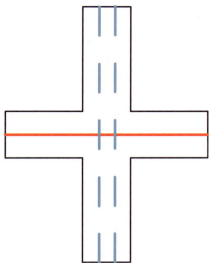

FIG. 1: Cut out the shape of a plus sign. Draw the horizontal and vertical cutting lines on both sides of the paper.

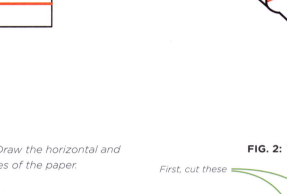

FIG. 2: Tape the short arms.

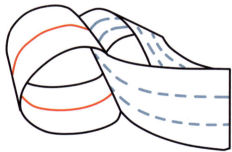

FIG. 3: Tape the long arms into a Möbius strip.

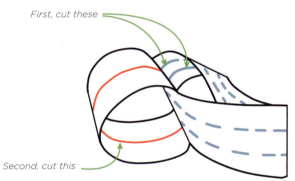

First, cut these

Second, cut this

FIG. 4: First cut the dotted lines, then cut the solid line.

FIG. 5: Before cutting the lines, guess the result!

TOPOLOGY: MIND-BENDING SHAPES

3

COLOR MAPS LIKE A MATHEMATICIAN

When you color a map, you're probably most interested in making it beautiful. When mathematicians talk about coloring a map, they're trying to figure out the fewest number of colors they can use so that no touching areas are the same color. Often, the "map" is not of a place—it's a picture with various regions to color. Mathematicians study map coloring to learn about efficiency and conflict resolution. Today, one important application of map coloring is for cell phone frequencies.

The *Four Color Theorem* says that you never need more than four colors for any map drawn on a flat piece of paper. It was the first mathematical proof using computers, and for many years some mathematicians didn't believe it qualified as a proof becasue they could not independently check the steps.

Find an old coloring book and see how few colors you can use to color a page, with no two colors touching.

LAB 12
MAP COLORING BASICS

Materials

✔ Printouts of the following maps from our website: **Checkerboard Map, Modified Checkerboard Map, Triangle Map 1, Triangle Map 2, Seven-Point Star Map, Modified Seven-Point Star Map, South America Map** (see page 125)

✔ Crayons, markers, or colored pencils (at least four colors)

✔ Four different colors of beads, counters, or other items that won't roll once placed on a piece of paper, or four colors of modeling clay

Welcome to the world of map coloring! In this lab, learn to use the fewest colors possible to fill in various maps.

HOW MANY COLORS?

1. Color the *Checkerboard Map* with as few colors as possible, making sure to use different colors for shapes that are next to each other. How many colors do you need **(fig. 1)**? You could use as many as nine colors but you only need two **(fig. 2)**. Actually, some kids might even use more than one color for a single square. That's pretty, but for this chapter, let's limit each region to a single color.

2. How many colors do you need for the *Modified Checkerboard Map*? Try it and see **(fig. 3)**.

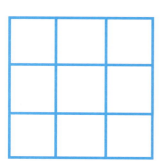

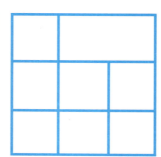

FIG. 1: *Color the checkerboard with as few colors as possible.*

FIG. 2: *You only need two colors.*

FIG. 3: *Color the modified checkerboard.*

Now that you've colored some maps, you'll see that our initial rule to use "as few colors as possible" wasn't precise enough. For the rest of this chapter, we'll use the following *map coloring rules*:

- Each region should get exactly one color.
- Use as few colors as possible.
- When two areas touch along a side, they need to be different colors.
- If areas only touch on a corner, it's okay for them to be the same color.

3. Try coloring *Triangle Map 1* **(fig. 4)** and *Triangle Map 2* **(fig. 5)**. The first one only needs two colors. The second one needs three.

> **Questions**
> - What were your strategies for figuring out which colors to use in order to have the fewest number possible?
> - Were there frequently used patterns in your colorings?

FIG. 4: *Triangle Map 1.*

FIG. 5: *Triangle Map 2.*

COLOR MAPS LIKE A MATHEMATICIAN

MAP COLORING BASICS, *continued*

4. Using our map coloring rules, color the *Seven-Point Star Map* **(fig. 6)** and the *Modified Seven-Point Star Map* **(fig. 7)**.

5. Using our map coloring rules and four colors of beads or modeling clay, plan how you'll color the *South America Map* **(fig. 8)**. Check out the time-saving tips on the right for ideas. Once you're happy with your plan, go ahead and color the pull-out on page 125.

TRY THIS!

As you fill in the South America Map, can you pinpoint why it can't be done in fewer than four colors?

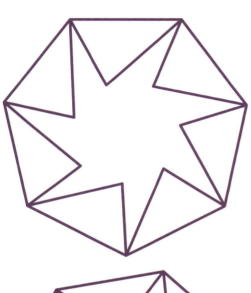

FIG. 6: *Color the Seven-Point Star Map.*

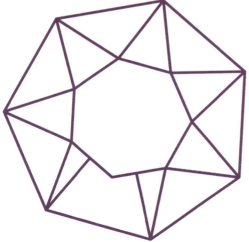

FIG. 7: *Color the Modified Seven-Point Star Map.*

FIG. 8: *Plan first and then color.*

48 MATH LAB FOR KIDS

SAVING TIME WHEN LOOKING FOR GOOD MAP COLORINGS

You may have noticed that if you just start coloring without planning, you might have to erase or start over a lot. So you're often better off planning which colors will go in which regions before coloring your masterpiece. Instead of fully coloring in the regions of a map, you could put a bead, a small piece of modeling clay, or even just a light pencil mark in each region to indicate which color that region will become. If your map is especially complicated or if you change your mind about a color for a region, this can save you a lot of time. All you have to do is use a new bead or piece of modeling clay, move a few beads or pieces of modeling clay, or erase your pencil marks instead of starting over. Once you have assigned a color to every region, you can confidently color your map knowing that you won't have to start over.

For example, the figure on the left shows a plan marked with beads, and the one on the right shows the plan implemented.

COLOR MAPS LIKE A MATHEMATICIAN

LAB 13: EFFICIENT MAP COLORING

Materials

- Printouts of the following from our website: **Partial U.S. Map, Bird Map, Abstract Map, Africa Map** (see page 126)
- Crayons, markers, or colored pencils (at least four colors)
- Four different colors of beads, counters, or modeling clay

Here you'll learn some techniques to efficiently color maps. Using the map coloring rules (page 47) and part of the map of the United States, we'll learn a famous technique to find a good map coloring. We're showing one way to color the map, but there are many other correct colorings.

COLOR WITH THE GREEDY ALGORITHM

1. Use red to color one region of the *Partial U.S. Map* **(fig. 1)**.

2. Color as many other regions as possible red. Don't forget that regions next to a red region can't be red **(fig. 2)**.

3. Once you cannot color any more regions red, color one region blue **(fig. 3)**.

4. Color as many other regions as you can blue **(fig. 4)**.

MATH FACT

What's the Greedy Algorithm?

This technique, where you color as much as you can with one color before moving on to another color, is called the *Greedy Algorithm*. Can you guess why?

FIG. 1: *Color one region red.*

FIG. 2: *Color as many other regions as possible red.*

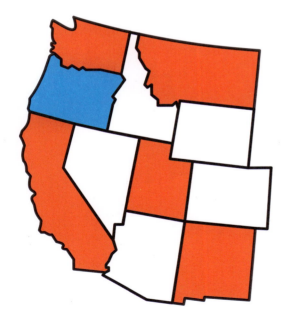

FIG. 3: *Once you cannot color any more regions red, color one region blue.*

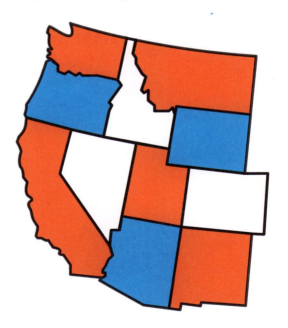

FIG. 4: *Color as many other regions as you can blue.*

COLOR MAPS LIKE A MATHEMATICIAN   51

EFFICIENT MAP COLORING, *continued*

5. Once you can't color any more regions blue, if the map isn't fully colored, color one region green **(fig. 5)**.

6. Color as many other regions as you can green **(fig. 6)**.

7. If the map still isn't fully colored, color any remaining regions yellow **(fig. 7)**.

8. You should be done at this point.

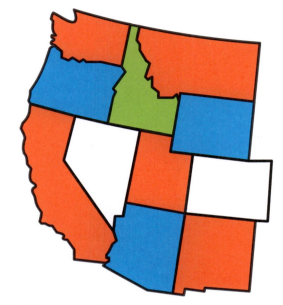

FIG. 5: *If the map isn't fully colored, color one region green.*

FIG. 6: *Color as many other regions as you can green.*

FIG. 7: *Color any remaining regions yellow.*

Planning Colors

Now try this technique on the *Bird Map*, *Abstract Map*, and *Africa Map* (see page 126). Use beads, modeling clay, or light pencil marks to plan your map's colors before you start. The Africa Map, in particular, will take careful planning. You can definitely color it with only four colors, so keep trying if you get stuck. If you have to start over a few times, it may make you feel better to learn that mathematicians often use computers to help them find a good coloring.

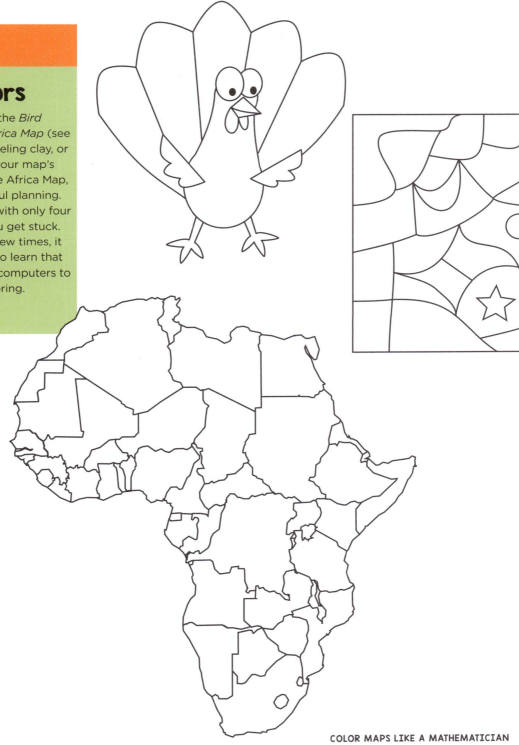

COLOR MAPS LIKE A MATHEMATICIAN

LAB 14: SQUIGGLE MAPS

Materials

- ✔ Pencil
- ✔ Several blank sheets of paper
- ✔ Crayons, markers, or colored pencils

MATH MEET
Draw Maps for Your Friends

Draw your own map and challenge your friends to color it using our map coloring rules! If you're not feeling artistic or just want to save time, you can get out a coloring book and treat any picture in the book as a map.

TRY THIS!

Every squiggle map can be fully colored with just two colors. Can you figure out why?

Any picture you draw with a pencil or pen can be thought of as a map. Learn to draw and color a map made from a single squiggly line.

DRAW A SQUIGGLE MAP

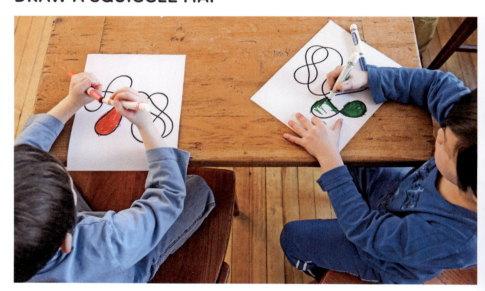

1. Put your pencil on a clean sheet of paper.

2. Draw a long, curving line that goes anywhere on the paper **(fig. 1)**. Do not take the pencil off the paper or go off an edge. (The big red dot shows where you started your squiggle. You don't need to draw a big dot on your picture.)

3. The line you are drawing can cross itself any number of times anywhere on the paper **(fig. 2)**.

4. Your map is finished when your pencil gets back to the starting point. You'll end up with a tangled squiggle **(fig. 3)**.

5. Using the techniques you learned in the previous labs, fill in your squiggle map with as few colors as possible **(fig. 4)**.

6. Try making and coloring more squiggle maps on your own.

FIG. 1: *Draw a long, curving line that goes anywhere on the paper.*

FIG. 2: *Your line can cross itself any number of times. Don't lift your pencil or go off an edge.*

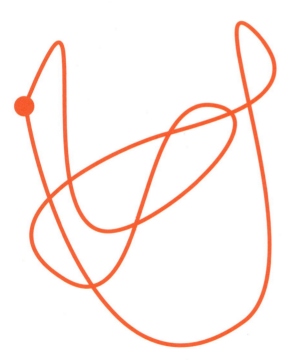

FIG. 3: *Get your pencil back to the starting point*

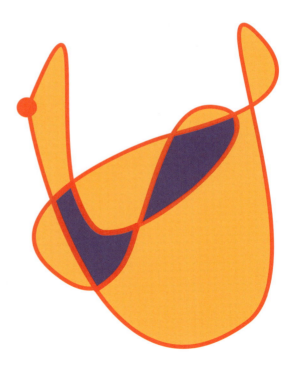

FIG. 4: *Fill in your squiggle map with as few colors as possible.*

COLOR MAPS LIKE A MATHEMATICIAN

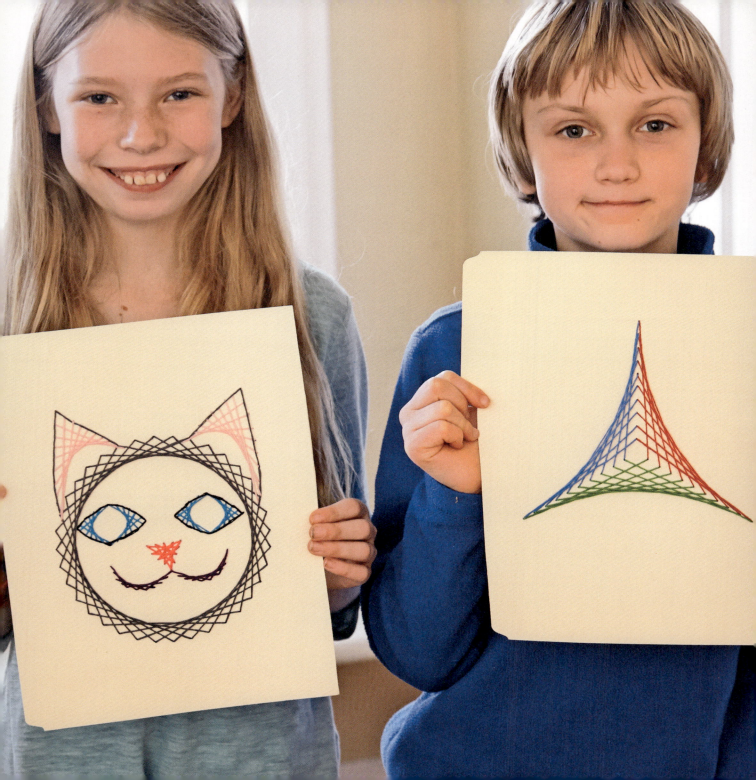

4

STITCHING CURVES

Sometimes equations are too hard to solve, even for professionals! For these problems, people invent methods that are easy to compute and approximate the solution. This branch of mathematics is called Numerical Analysis. These numerical algorithms are usually done on a computer, and by doing more calculations you can make your approximate solution as good as you need. Curve stitching is a way to approximate a curve by drawing only straight lines, without any computation needed. The closer you draw the lines together, the better the approximation to the curve you make. We can use the same technique to make a variety of curves and shapes that can be turned into beautiful art.

Can you draw a curve (or something that looks like a curve) using only straight lines?

LAB 15
DRAWING PARABOLAS

Materials

- Pencil
- Unlined paper or graph paper
- Ruler
- Compass (optional)

Learn to create a parabola—a type of curve—using only straight lines.

GRAPH A PARABOLA WITH DIFFERENT ANGLES

1. Draw two lines that intersect to form a *right angle* (the angle formed at the corner of a square, also known as a *90-degree angle*). This is easy to do with graph paper, or you can use the corner of a book as a drawing guide.

2. Make six evenly spaced marks along the lines. With graph paper, space the marks every five squares apart, or you can use a ruler to measure every inch (2.5 cm) and make a mark. Number the marks along the bottom and side of the lines as shown **(fig. 1)**.

3. Using your ruler, connect the two points labeled with the number 1 with a straight line **(fig. 2)**.

4. Next, connect the two points labeled with the number 2 with a straight line **(fig. 3)**.

5. Repeat steps 3 and 4 by connecting each of the remaining points that have the same number. You should end up with a curve that looks like the one in **fig. 4**. This curve approximates a parabola. The more straight lines you use, the smoother the curve will appear (see "What's Going On?," page 60).

MATH FACT
What's a Parabola?

A *parabola* is the U-shaped curve made by the intersection of a cone and a plane (see below). Parabolas can be found in lots of places in the real world. When you throw a ball, the path it travels is a parabola. Extended into three dimensions, a curved surface whose cross-sections are parabolas (a *paraboloid*) is used in telescopes to focus light to a single point.

MATH LAB FOR KIDS

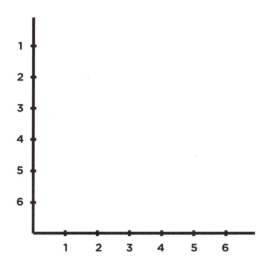

FIG. 1: *Draw two lines at a right angle. Mark each line with six evenly spaced marks. Number the marks as shown.*

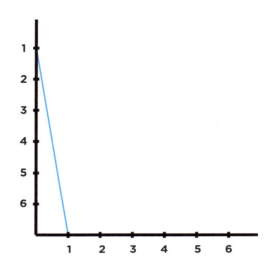

FIG. 2: *Use a ruler to connect the two points numbered 1.*

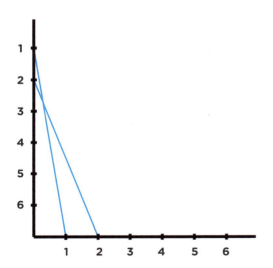

FIG. 3: *Connect the two points numbered 2.*

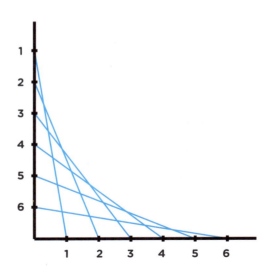

FIG. 4: *Connect the remaining points with the same number.*

STITCHING CURVES

DRAWING PARABOLAS, *continued*

What's Going On?

The more points you start with along each line, the closer your approximation will be to a real parabola. Try drawing a more accurate parabola by starting with twelve marks along each side instead of six and compare your results. Imagine how close you could come to an exact parabola if you used fifty points along each line, or a hundred!

6. This method of graphing a parabola works with any angle. Try drawing curves using starting lines in an *acute angle* (an angle that's narrower than a right angle, or less than 90 degrees) **(figs. 5 and 6)** and at an *obtuse angle* (one that's wider than a right angle, or greater than 90 degrees) **(figs. 7 and 8)**.

7. As you graph your parabolas, notice how the shape of the curve changes when the angle of the starting lines changes. With an acute angle, the shape of the curve compresses. With an obtuse angle, the shape of the curve expands or stretches.

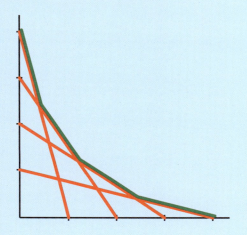

Two parabolas, one graphed with four marks along each line (top) and the other with twelve marks (bottom). The curve that each one makes is shown in green.

60   MATH LAB FOR KIDS

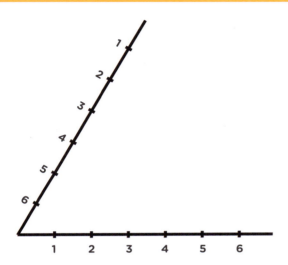

FIG. 5: *You can graph a parabola on an acute angle (less than 90 degrees).*

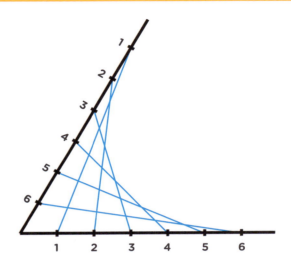

FIG. 6: *The shape of the parabola compresses with an acute angle.*

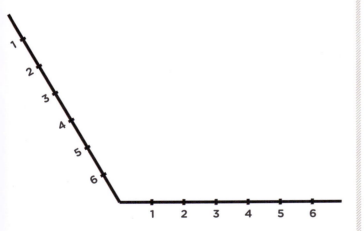

FIG. 7: *You can also graph one on an obtuse angle (greater than 90 degrees).*

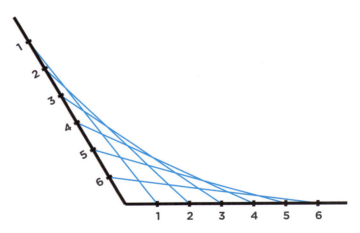

FIG. 8: *The shape of the parabola expands with an obtuse angle.*

STITCHING CURVES 61

LAB 16: STITCHING STARS

Materials

- Pencil and eraser
- Manila folder or very lightweight cardboard
- Ruler
- Pushpin
- Corrugated cardboard or a bath towel
- Scissors
- Thread (embroidery thread, yarn, or other thick thread)
- Blunt needle
- Tape (clear tape or masking tape)

TRY THIS!
Can you use this method to make a three-point star or a five-point star?

Using a needle and thread, combine parabolas into beautiful stars.

STITCH A STAR

1. Using a pencil, lightly draw two lines in the shape of a plus sign on your manila folder. (Don't press too hard; you're going to erase them later.) Using your ruler, make even marks from the center point and moving outward along each line **(fig. 1)**.

2. Using the pushpin, carefully poke a hole at each mark on your folder. This is easier to do if you put your folder over something that you can push pins into safely, like a piece of corrugated cardboard or a thick, folded towel.

3. Lightly number two of the lines as shown **(fig. 2)**.

4. Cut a piece of thread about the length of your arm and thread it onto your needle.

5. Starting from the back of your folder, push the needle through the hole you labeled #1. That is at the tip of your star. As you pull the thread through the hole, stop when there are a few inches still sticking through and tape the end of the thread down on the BACK of the folder very securely. Tug on the thread a little to make sure it won't slip through **(fig. 3)**.

6. Your needle should be on the front side of your folder now. Push the needle down through the other hole marked #1 to make a long stitch. Your thread should connect the two dots, just like you did with pencil in Lab 15.

7. Starting on the back side of your folder again, push the needle through the hole right next to it, which should be hole #2, making a short stitch. Then, from the front side, you can make another long stitch to connect both #2 holes **(fig. 4)**.

8. Continue like this for the rest of the holes. You should have long stitches on the front side of your folder, and short stitches on the back. When you run out of thread, tape the end down on the back of your folder, cut another piece of thread, thread your needle, and keep going! When you've finished your curve, tape the end of the thread on the back of the folder and trim any long ends **(fig. 5)**.

9. Stitch the other three parabolas in the same way to finish your four-pointed star! You can number the other axes if you need to. Experiment with using different colors for your lines **(fig. 6)**.

10. Gently erase any visible pencil marks.

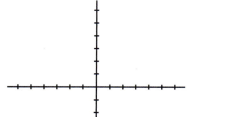

FIG. 1: *Draw a plus sign. With a ruler, make even marks along each line. Use a pushpin to make a hole at each mark.*

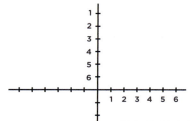

FIG. 2: *Lightly number two of the lines.*

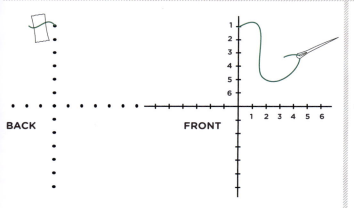

FIG. 3: *Push the needle through the back of hole #1. Tape the last few inches of the thread to the back of the folder.*

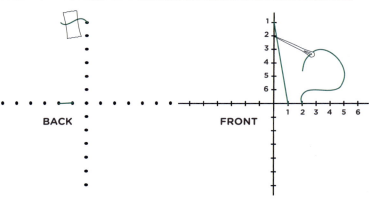

FIG. 4: *Make a short stitch through the back of hole #2. From the front, connect the two #2 holes with another long stitch.*

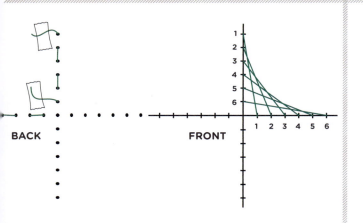

FIG. 5: *Continue like this for the rest of the holes.*

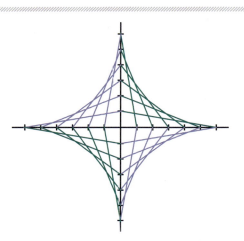

FIG. 6: *Stitch the other three parabolas in the same way.*

STITCHING CURVES

LAB 17
CREATIVE CURVES

Materials

- Pencil and eraser
- Manila folder or very lightweight cardboard (optional)
- Can or cup (optional)
- Ruler
- Pushpin
- Corrugated cardboard or a bath towel
- Scissors
- Thread (embroidery thread, yarn, or other thick thread)
- Blunt needle
- Tape (clear tape or masking tape)

Either by drawing or by stitching, make curves other than parabolas using only straight lines.

DRAW OR STITCH A CURVE

1. Draw a circle or an oval shape. You can draw it freehand, use a can or cup as a stencil, or construct a circle or an ellipse using string and tape (see chapter 1, Labs 5 and 7). If you want to draw the shapes with a pencil, you can use plain unlined paper. If you want to stitch the shapes with a needle and thread, draw the circle on a manila folder.

2. The trickiest part of this is making the evenly spaced marks around your shape. One good strategy is to use a ruler and make a pencil mark every inch or centimeter. Some marks probably won't be even, but that's okay **(fig. 1)**. Can you think of any other ways you might try to make evenly spaced marks?

3. Once you've drawn the marks, choose which two to connect first. It is best to choose marks that are neither right next to each other nor right across from each other. Connect the two marks you chose, either by drawing with your pencil and ruler, or by stitching it with thread and a blunt needle **(fig. 2)**. To use thread, see steps 3–5 in Lab 16.

4. Move over one mark clockwise from the line you drew, and connect it to the mark that is one mark past your previous connection in a clockwise direction **(fig. 3)**. If your first two marks were ten marks apart from each other, your next two marks should also be ten marks apart.

5. Go around the whole shape until you get back to where you started. When you are finished, each mark should have two lines coming out of it **(fig. 4)**.

MEET THE MATHEMATICIAN
MARY EVEREST BOOLE

Mary Everest Boole (1832–1916, England) was the inventor of curve stitching. She taught herself calculus using her father's books, and learned more by corresponding with famous mathematicians. She started her career as a librarian and then became a teacher of math and science. Her hands-on methods, encouragement of critical thinking, and careful use of repetition still influence classrooms today.

MATH LAB FOR KIDS

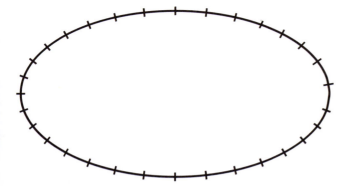

FIG. 1: *Draw a circle or an oval shape. Make evenly spaced marks around your shape. You might notice that some marks are a bit uneven. That's okay—it'll still look great!*

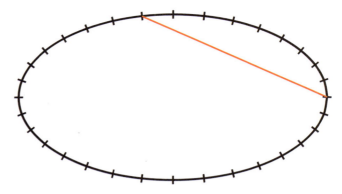

FIG. 2: *Connect two marks, either by drawing with a pencil and ruler or by stitching with thread.*

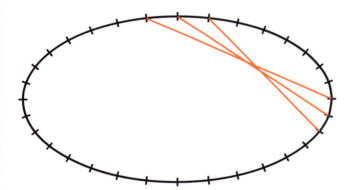

FIG. 3: *Connect dots in a clockwise direction.*

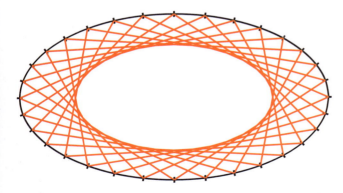

FIG. 4: *Keep going until you get back to the dot you started on.*

TRY THIS!

You can use this technique with lots of shapes—ovals, triangles, and other polygons, moon shapes, fish, dinosaurs, rocketships, etc. Try some out! Be creative in how you connect your lines. See what patterns you can create to enhance your artwork. This is a great time to experiment with colors, too.

STITCHING CURVES

5
FANTASTIC FRACTALS

A *fractal* is a shape that is similar to itself no matter how far you zoom in on one particular part.

Fractals occur in nature, such as in ice crystals freezing on a window. They are interesting to mathematicians and scientists as part of Chaos Theory and the study of patterns found in nature where parts are similar to the whole. For example, look at the ferns on the right. Notice how the blue branch of the fern looks like a smaller copy of the green fern, and the purple portion of the fern has a very similar shape to both the whole green fern and the blue branch.

Understanding fractals has helped research in the stock market, fluids, astronomy, and weather. Fractals are also interesting to artists simply because they are beautiful.

Can you think of other examples of self-similar objects?

LAB 18: DRAW A SIERPINSKI TRIANGLE

Materials

- ✔ Paper
- ✔ Pencil
- ✔ Ruler or measuring tape
- ✔ **Equilateral Triangle Template** (*see page 127*)
- ✔ Crayons or markers in several colors

The Sierpinski triangle is an example of a fractal.

FROM EQUILATERAL TO SIERPINSKI TRIANGLE

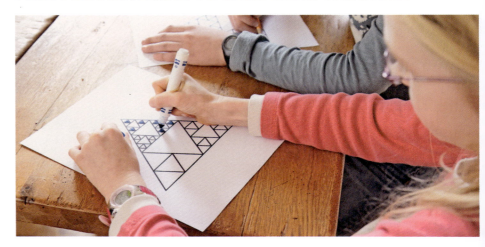

1. Draw a large *equilateral triangle* (see page 26) with 6-inch (15 cm) sides **(fig. 1)**. You can do this by following the directions in Lab 6. For a shortcut, you can trace the *Equilateral Triangle Template* on page 127.

2. Use your ruler to measure the length of each edge of the triangle and put a dot in the center of each edge **(fig. 2)**. Mathematicians call this dot a *midpoint*. (Younger children may wish to eyeball the midpoint.)

3. Connect each midpoint to create a new triangle, pointing down, inside the first triangle **(fig. 3)**. Our original triangle is now divided into four smaller triangles **(fig. 4)**. By definition, the center triangle is not part of the Sierpinski triangle—only the outer three triangles are.

4. Now we'll divide each of the three smaller triangles like we did before. Mark the midpoints of the sides of the three outer triangles **(fig. 5)**.

5. Connect the new midpoints **(fig. 6)**.

6. Continue adding midpoints and creating new triangles. When you're done, color it in however you like. Yours is probably prettier than ours **(fig. 7)**.

Congratulations! You made a Sierpinski triangle.

MATH LAB FOR KIDS

  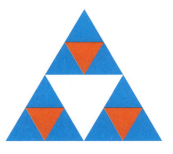 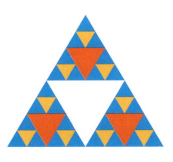

Sierpinski triangles.

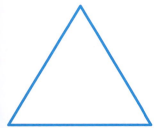 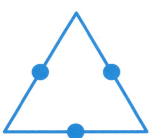 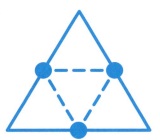 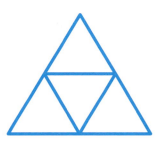

FIG. 1: *Draw an equilateral triangle.*

FIG. 2: *Put a dot in the center of each edge.*

FIG. 3: *Connect each set of midpoints.*

FIG. 4: *We now have four smaller triangles.*

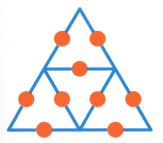 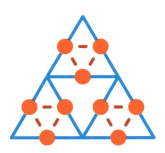  

FIG. 5: *Mark the midpoints of the sides of the three outer triangles.*

FIG. 6: *Connect the new midpoints.*

FIG. 7: *Continue adding midpoints and creating new triangles. When you're done, color it in however you like.*

FANTASTIC FRACTALS

LAB 19: BUILD A SIERPINSKI TRIANGLE

Materials

- ✔ Paper in at least three colors
- ✔ Pencil
- ✔ Ruler or measuring tape
- ✔ **Equilateral Triangle Template** (*see page 127*)
- ✔ Scissors
- ✔ Large piece of paper (poster, butcher, packing, or other large paper—optional)
- ✔ Glue or tape

Here is another way to create a colorful Sierpinski triangle. This activity is great with many kids.

MAKE A SIERPINSKI TRIANGLE

1. Using only one color of paper (we used purple), draw three large equilateral triangles with 6-inch (15 cm) sides. You can do this by following the directions in Lab 6. For a shortcut, you can use the *Equilateral Triangle Template* on page 127 as a stencil.

2. Cut them out.

3. Arrange them in a Sierpinski triangle **(fig. 1)**.

4. Using a different color (we used blue), make a fourth triangle the same size as the triangles from step 1.

5. Cut the new triangle into four smaller triangles by connecting the midpoints of the three sides and then cutting each side **(fig. 2)**. (For a reminder on how to find the midpoint, see Lab 18.)

6. Arrange three of the new smaller triangles onto your existing Sierpinski triangle, using glue or tape to hold the smaller triangles in place **(fig. 3)**.

7. Repeat these steps with new colors as many times as you like **(fig. 4)**.

8. *Optional*: If you build a lot of Sierpinski triangles, you can arrange them into a giant one! If you have a large piece of paper, glue or tape the triangles there to hold them down. Start from the bottom left corner so you can add more layers later in the *Math Meet* on page 73 **(fig. 5)**.

FIG. 1: *Arrange your triangles in a Sierpinski triangle.*

FIG. 2: *Cut the new triangle into four smaller triangles.*

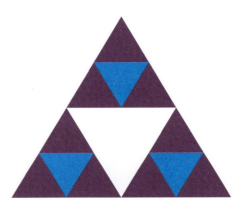

FIG. 3: *Tape or glue three of the new smaller triangles onto your existing Sierpinski triangle.*

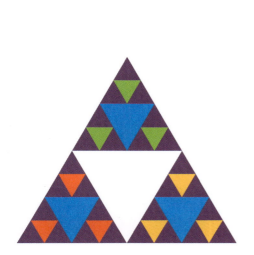

FIG. 4: *Our final Sierpinski triangle.*

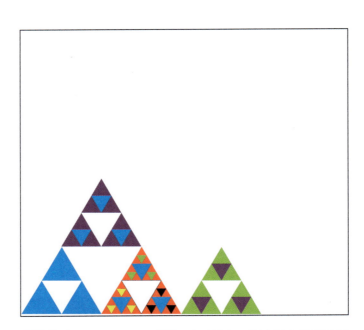

FIG. 5: *Arrange your small Sierpinski triangles into a giant one.*

FANTASTIC FRACTALS 71

BUILD A SIERPINSKI TRIANGLE, *continued*

MATH FACT
Sierpinski Triangle's Area

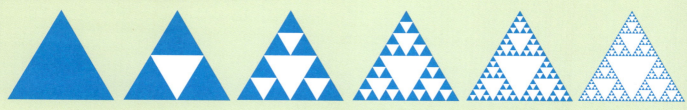

The *area* of an object is the amount of space it takes up. Though we created beautiful works of art in the previous labs, the formal definition of a Sierpinski triangle is just the colored triangles in the illustration above. (Thus the white space is *not* part of the area we will calculate below.)

- The area of the first triangle in Lab 18 is approximately 16 square inches (41 square centimeters). Mathematicians use the ≈ sign to mean "approximately equal." It's like an equal sign but not quite.

- In the next step, we divide our original triangle into four equal pieces and remove the one in the middle. If our original triangle had an area of 16, and we divided it into four pieces, how big would the smaller triangles be? Can you figure out why the area of our new Sierpinski is 12 square inches (30 square centimeters)?

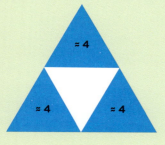

- Every time you add a new set of smaller triangles to your Sierpinski triangle, the area of the resulting Sierpinski triangle is three-quarters the area of the previous *iteration*. That's because we divided the previous triangle into four pieces and removed the middle one. (An iteration is one complete pass through a set of steps that gets repeated. For example, your bottle of shampoo probably says to "lather, rinse, repeat" as often as necessary until your hair is clean. One lather/rinse cycle is one iteration. If you lather and rinse twice, that's two iterations.)

If we keep subdividing triangles and taking the center part away forever, we'd end up with a shape that has no area at all!

72   MATH LAB FOR KIDS

MATH MEET
Build a Huge Sierpinski Triangle

Arrange as many triangles as you have from Lab 19 or cut new 6-inch (15 cm) ones to form a huge Sierpinski triangle. Use the method learned in Lab 19—it's best if you attach them to a large piece of paper or poster board so that they don't move around. As a bonus, you will be able to hang your finished Sierpinski triangle somewhere for all to admire. If you like, send us a picture for inclusion on our website.

TRY THIS!
Sierpinski Activities

- What is the *perimeter* (length of the edges) of a Sierpinski triangle?
- How many triangles are in a Sierpinski triangle after one iteration? Two? Three? Ten? Can you find a pattern?
- What would a *Sierpinski pyramid* (a three-dimensional Sierpinski triangle) look like?

FANTASTIC FRACTALS

LAB 20: DRAW A KOCH SNOWFLAKE

Materials

- Paper
- Pencil (not pen)
- Ruler or measuring tape
- **Equilateral Triangle Template** (*see page 127*)

One of the earliest fractals discovered and described is the Koch snowflake.

MAKE A KOCH SNOWFLAKE

1. Draw an equilateral triangle with all sides measuring 6 inches (15 cm) **(fig. 1)**. You can do this by following the directions in Lab 6. For a shortcut, you can trace the *Equilateral Triangle Template* on page 127.

2. We're going to divide each side into three equal *segments* (the part of a line between two points). Draw a mark at 2 inches (5 cm) and at 4 inches (10 cm) from each *vertex* (corner) of the triangle **(fig. 2)**. (Younger kids may eyeball their marks approximately one-third and two-thirds of the distance from each corner.)

3. The space between your two marks is the base of a new equilateral triangle. Draw it so that it points outward **(figs. 3 and 4)**.

4. Erase the base of the three new triangles you drew in step 3 **(fig. 5)**.

KEEP YOUR KOCH SNOWFLAKE FOR LAB 22!

MATH LAB FOR KIDS

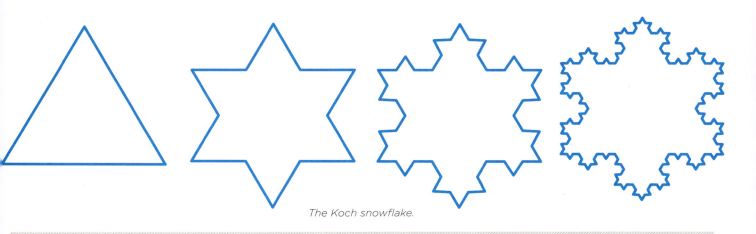

The Koch snowflake.

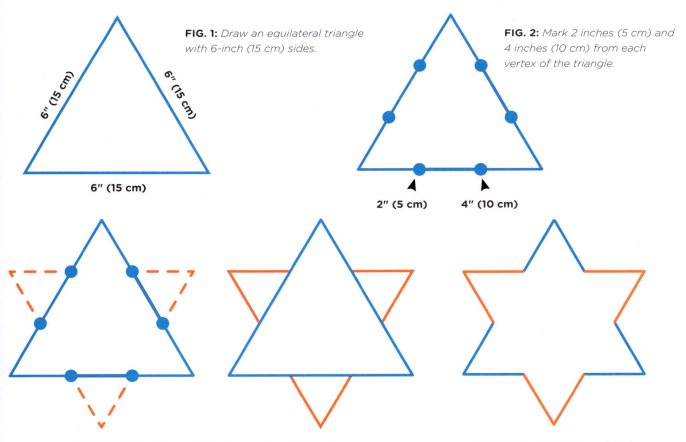

FIG. 1: *Draw an equilateral triangle with 6-inch (15 cm) sides.*

FIG. 2: *Mark 2 inches (5 cm) and 4 inches (10 cm) from each vertex of the triangle.*

FIGS. 3 AND 4: *Connect the two marks with the base of an equilateral triangle, pointing it outward.*

FIG. 5: *Erase the base of each new triangle.*

FANTASTIC FRACTALS

DRAW A KOCH SNOWFLAKE, *continued*

FIG. 6: *Divide each side of the shape from step 4 into three equal segments. Repeat step 3 using these marks.*

5. Divide each side of the shape from step 4 into three segments of equal length by placing two marks on each side. Draw an equilateral triangle that points outward and whose base connects the two marks from the previous step **(fig. 6)**.

6. Erase the base of each new equilateral triangle **(fig. 7)**.

7. Repeat steps 5 and 6 as many times as you like (**fig. 8** shows a partial example).

8. Congratulations, you've drawn a Koch snowflake **(fig. 9)**!

FIG. 7: *Erase the base of each new equilateral triangle.*

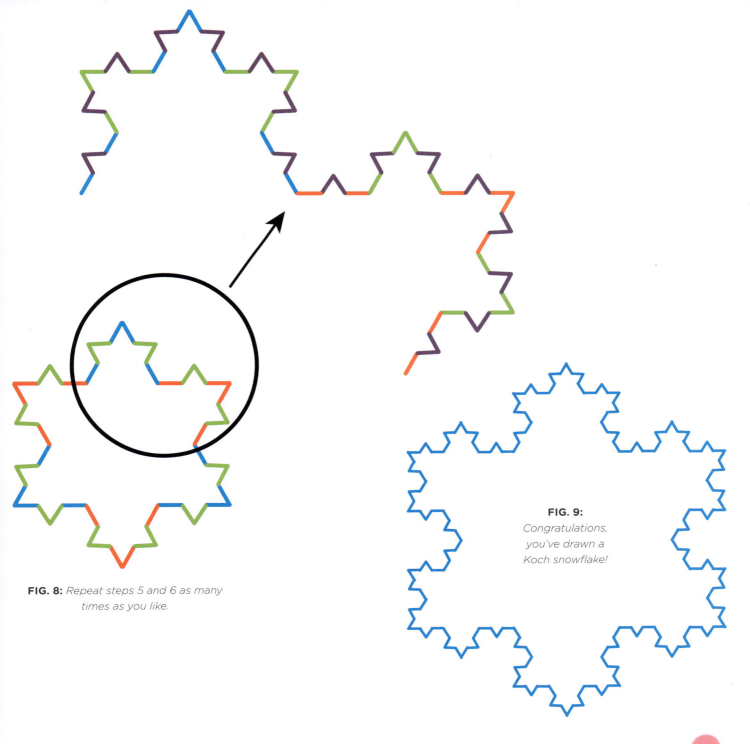

FIG. 8: Repeat steps 5 and 6 as many times as you like.

FIG. 9: Congratulations, you've drawn a Koch snowflake!

FANTASTIC FRACTALS

LAB 21: DRAW A SQUARE FRACTAL SNOWFLAKE

Materials

- Paper
- Pencil (not pen)
- Ruler or measuring tape

Fractal snowflakes aren't always based on the shape of a triangle. What happens when you use the shape of a square as the base?

DRAW A SQUARE SNOWFLAKE

1. Draw a square. Divide each side of the square into three segments of equal length **(fig. 1)**.

2. Draw a square pointing outward, whose base is the middle segment of each side as marked in step 1 **(fig. 2)**.

3. Erase the middle segment you used as the base of the square you just added **(fig. 3)**.

4. Repeat steps 2 through 4 as many times as you like **(fig. 4)**.

TRY THIS!

Create Your Own Fractal Snowflake

Can you think of another shape you could turn into a Koch-like snowflake? Try it! Don't forget to name it. A snowflake named after you sounds nice, doesn't it?

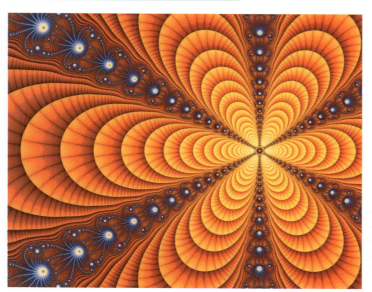

A portion of the Julia set fractal, based on French mathematician Gaston Julia's work (1893–1978).

78 MATH LAB FOR KIDS

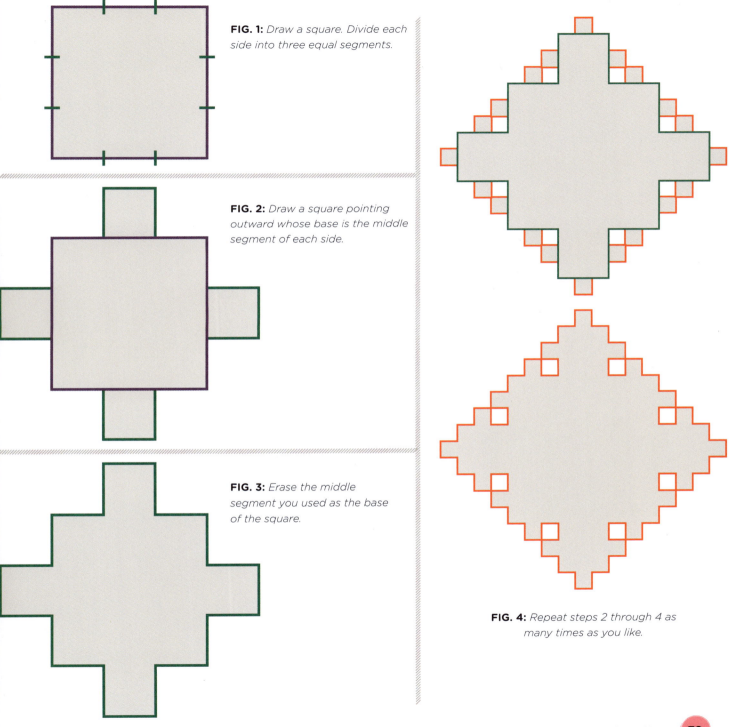

FIG. 1: *Draw a square. Divide each side into three equal segments.*

FIG. 2: *Draw a square pointing outward whose base is the middle segment of each side.*

FIG. 3: *Erase the middle segment you used as the base of the square.*

FIG. 4: *Repeat steps 2 through 4 as many times as you like.*

FANTASTIC FRACTALS

LAB 22: EXPLORE THE KOCH SNOWFLAKE'S PERIMETER

Materials

- ✔ Koch snowflake from Lab 20
- ✔ Ruler or measuring tape
- ✔ Paper

The perimeter is the distance around the edge of a shape. Can you find the perimeter of a Koch snowflake?

FIND THE PERIMETER

1. Use your ruler to measure the length of each side of the triangle from step 1 of Lab 20. If you add them up, you'll measure what mathematicians call the *perimeter*. Write down the perimeter of the original triangle **(fig. 1)**. You got 18 inches (45 cm), right? Because the perimeter is 6 + 6 + 6 inches (15 + 15 + 15 cm).

2. Measure and write down the perimeter of the shape from step 4 of Lab 20 **(fig. 2)**.

3. Measure and write down the perimeter of the shape from step 6 of Lab 20 **(fig. 3)**.

4. If you added more sides to your Koch snowflake, measure and write down those perimeters.

5. What do you notice? Can you guess what will happen to the perimeter of a Koch snowflake if you keep adding sides forever?

What's Going On?

In each step, we add more and more edges to the Koch snowflake. The more edges you add, the bigger the perimeter gets. So if you keep adding edges forever, the perimeter will keep getting bigger forever. It turns out that the perimeter of a Koch snowflake is infinity. Amazing!

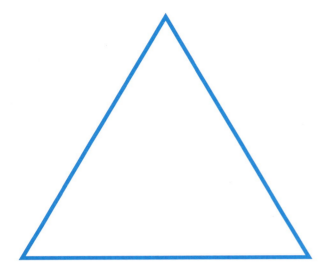

FIG. 1: *Measure the length of each side of the original triangle from step 1 of Lab 20.*

FIG. 2: *Measure and write down the perimeter of the shape from step 4, fig. 5 of Lab 20.*

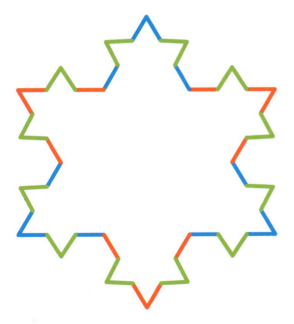

FIG. 3: *Measure and write down the perimeter of the shape from step 6, fig. 7 of Lab 20.*

TRY THIS!
Area of a Koch Snowflake

Can you figure out about how much space a Koch snowflake takes up?

HINTS:

- You should be looking for an approximate answer, not an exact answer.
- If you drew an infinite Koch snowflake, would you need a bigger sheet of paper?
- What shape will a Koch snowflake fit inside?

FANTASTIC FRACTALS

6

TERRIFIC TANGRAMS

Tangrams were invented in China hundreds of years ago. Legend has it that a Chinese emperor's servant dropped a precious tile that broke into seven pieces. As the servant attempted to reassemble the tile, he discovered he could create many beautiful shapes from the seven pieces.

Tangram puzzles are a bit like jigsaw puzzles, except you always use the same seven pieces to create different shapes. In addition to being fun, solving tangram puzzles builds problem-solving skills, develops geometric intuition, and improves pattern recognition and design abilities.

How can the same seven pieces make a square and also a square that is missing some space inside (like the pictures below)?

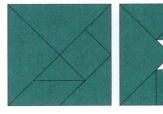

LAB 23
TANGRAM BASICS

Materials

✔ Set of tangrams

Note: *There is a set of tangrams on page 129 that you can pull out and cut up. If you want a more durable set, they're easy to buy online.*

Tangram puzzles always use the same seven pieces to make a picture.

STARTER TANGRAMS

See solutions on page 135.

1. Can you make a bat with your seven tangrams **(fig. 1)**?

2. Can you make a giraffe with your seven tangrams **(fig. 2)**?

3. Can you make a helicopter with your seven tangrams **(fig. 3)**?

4. Can you make a turtle with your seven tangrams **(fig. 4)**?

5. Can you make a rabbit with your seven tangrams **(fig. 5)**?

RULES FOR TANGRAMS

1. Use all seven tangram pieces (also called *tans*) for every puzzle.

2. Try different arrangements of the pieces to exactly match the picture.

3. You may have to flip the pieces over to solve the puzzles.

4. If you are having trouble, print out a full-size version of the puzzle from our website so the tangram pieces will fit inside. This will make the puzzles easier to solve.

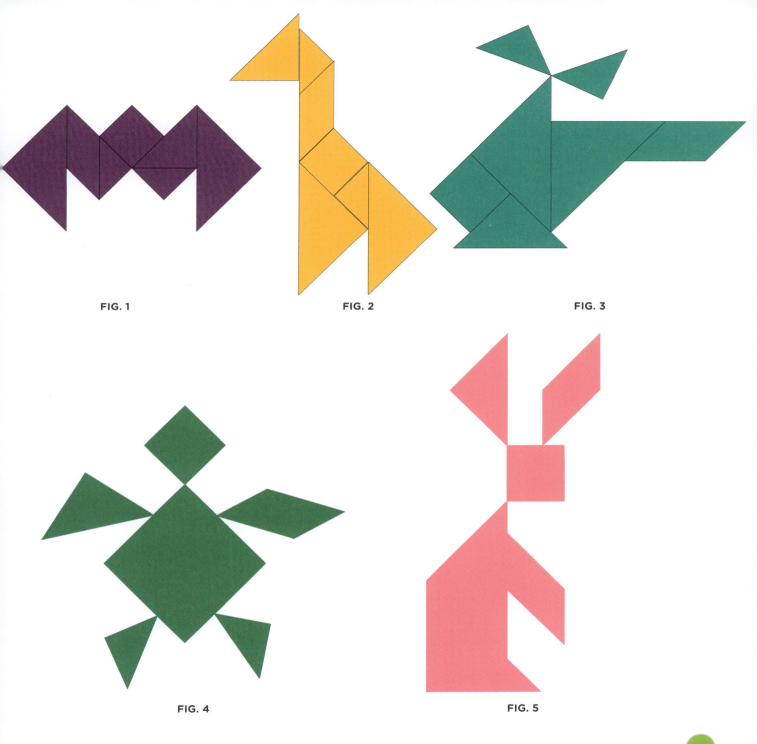

FIG. 1
FIG. 2
FIG. 3
FIG. 4
FIG. 5

TERRIFIC TANGRAMS

LAB 24
TEASER TANGRAMS

Materials

✔ Set of tangrams (*see page 129*)

You can print out full-size versions of these puzzles from our website.

What else can you make with your set of tangrams?

NEXT-LEVEL TANGRAMS

See solutions on page 135.

1. Can you make a cat with your seven tangrams **(fig. 1)**?

2. Can you make a dog with your seven tangrams **(fig. 2)**?

3. Can you make a candle with your seven tangrams **(fig. 3)**?

4. Can you make a rocket with your seven tangrams **(fig. 4)**?

5. Can you make a square with your seven tangrams **(fig. 5)**?

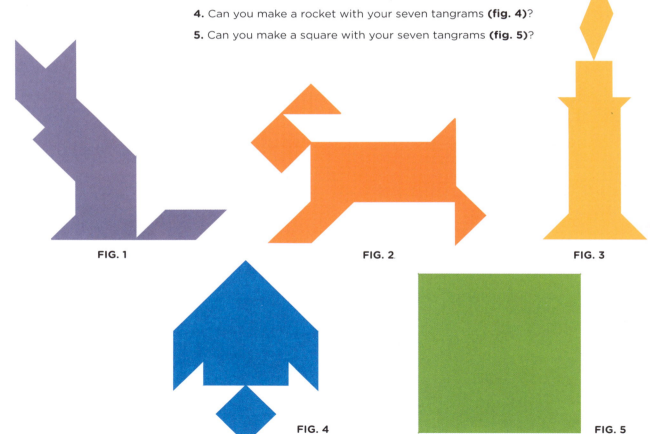

FIG. 1

FIG. 2

FIG. 3

FIG. 4

FIG. 5

MATH LAB FOR KIDS

MATH MEET
Tangrams Party

Making your own tangram puzzle is easier than you think. Here are two methods.

METHOD 1
1. Move your tangrams around until you find a shape you like.
2. Trace the outline.
3. Name your tangram.
4. Challenge your friend(s) to solve it!

METHOD 2
1. Think of a shape you would like to make and see if you and your friend(s) can make it. For example, can you make all 26 letters of the alphabet or the numbers 0 through 9 with your tangrams? What about a triangle?
2. Once you have a solution you like, trace the outline.
3. Trade puzzles with your friend(s) and solve each other's tangrams.

Materials
- ✔ Set of tangrams (see page 129)
- ✔ Pencil
- ✔ Paper
- ✔ At least two people

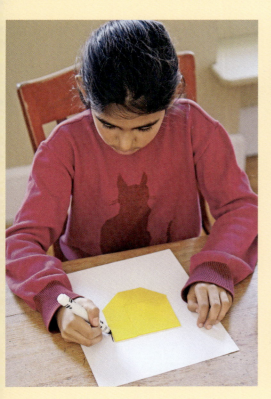

TERRIFIC TANGRAMS

LAB 25
TOUGHER TANGRAMS

Materials
✔ 2 sets of tangrams (*see page 129*)

Let's take tangrams to a whole new level! If you get stuck, print out the full-size versions from our website.

TANGRAMS CHALLENGE

1. Can you make a house with your seven tangrams **(fig. 1)**?

2. Can you make a boat with your seven tangrams **(fig. 2)**?

3. Can you make an arrow with your seven tangrams **(fig. 3)**?

4. Can you make a double arrow with your seven tangrams **(fig. 4)**?

5. Can you make these two bridges **(fig. 5)**? (You'll need a set of tangrams for each bridge.)

6. Can you make these monks using your seven tangrams **(fig. 6)**? This puzzle was created by English mathematician Henry Ernest Dudeny (1857–1930). Two monks look the same, but one is missing a foot. (You'll need a full set of seven tangrams for each monk.)

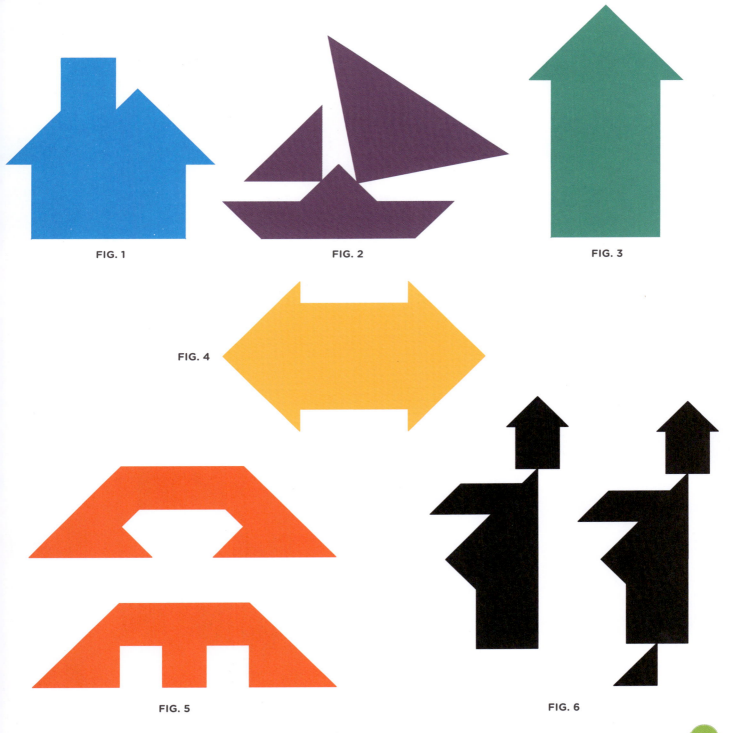

FIG. 1
FIG. 2
FIG. 3
FIG. 4
FIG. 5
FIG. 6

TERRIFIC TANGRAMS

TOOTHPICK PUZZLES

Toothpick puzzles (sometimes called matchstick puzzles) ask you to rearrange a given pattern of sticks into a second pattern according to a set of rules. They range from easy to very difficult, and are great brainteasers to encourage mathematical thinking—playing with ideas and seeing what comes out.

In addition to being fun, these puzzles build skills in rule-following, recognizing shapes, and counting. Because they are well suited to trial-and-error techniques, they can be a great tool to build problem-solving confidence, because you can just keep trying different solutions until you find one that works. The willingness to keep trying things when you don't know the answer is one of the most important mathematical skills there is.

How many triangles can you find in this image?
(*Hint*: The answer is greater than six!)

LAB 26: STARTER TOOTHPICK PUZZLES

Materials

- Toothpicks, matchsticks, or craft sticks

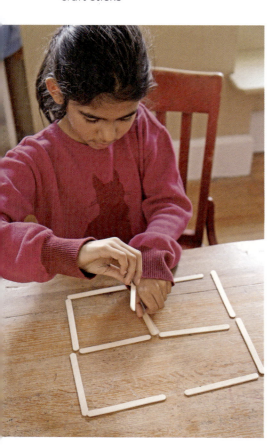

Learn to solve toothpick puzzles. Start with your toothpicks as shown in the figures. Then follow the instructions to transform the shapes.

ACTIVITY 1: PRACTICE PUZZLE

Hint: If a puzzle doesn't say that the squares or triangles need to be exactly the same size, they can be different sizes!

1. Remove two sticks from the puzzle in **fig. 1** to leave two squares.
2. The resulting shape has exactly two squares **(fig. 2)**—but they overlap **(fig. 3)**!

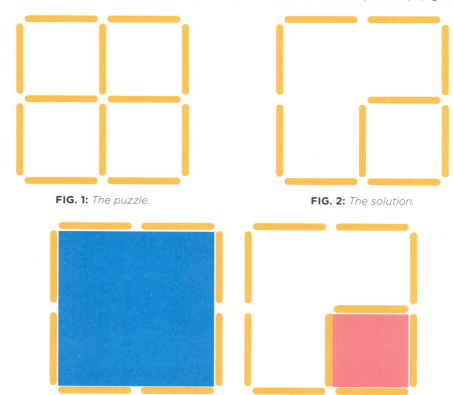

FIG. 1: *The puzzle.*   **FIG. 2:** *The solution.*

FIG. 3: *Two overlapping squares.*

92   MATH LAB FOR KIDS

ACTIVITY 2: STARTER PUZZLES

For solutions, see page 136.

1. Move two sticks to create two equal-size triangles **(fig. 4)**.
2. Move two sticks to make two equal-size squares **(fig. 5)**.
3. Start with five triangles. (Can you find them all?) Remove two sticks to leave exactly two triangles **(fig. 6)**.
4. Move three sticks to create five squares **(fig. 7)**.

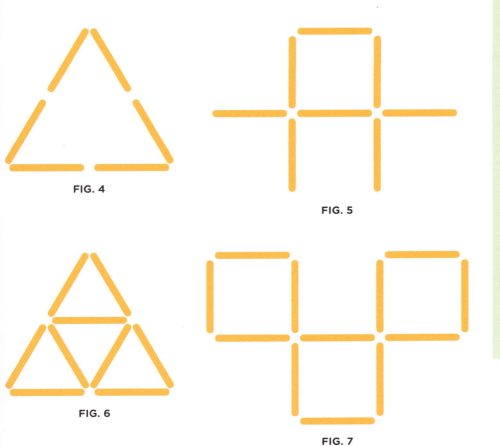

FIG. 4

FIG. 5

FIG. 6

FIG. 7

MATH TECHNIQUE
Trial and Error

This technique helps you solve a puzzle when you don't even know where to start! When you aren't sure how to begin solving a problem, use *trial and error.*

This problem-solving method involves trying something—anything—even if you don't think it will work, and then looking carefully at the result to see what happened. If it isn't what you wanted, go back to the beginning, and try something different. Keep trying things (and keep carefully looking at the result!) until you either find the solution or begin to get an idea of how the problem works, which may lead to a more efficient way to solve it.

For example, if a toothpick puzzle says "remove two sticks" to produce a particular result, start by just picking up any two sticks from the puzzle. What shapes are you left with? Could this be the solution to the puzzle? If not, put the sticks back, and try picking up two different sticks. Keep trying until you succeed!

TOOTHPICK PUZZLES

TOOTHPICK PUZZLES: THE NEXT LEVEL

Materials

✓ Toothpicks, matchsticks, or craft sticks
✓ Bead or penny, for fish puzzle

These puzzles are a little trickier! Start with your toothpicks as shown in the figures. Then follow the instructions to transform the shapes.

TRY MORE COMPLEX PUZZLES

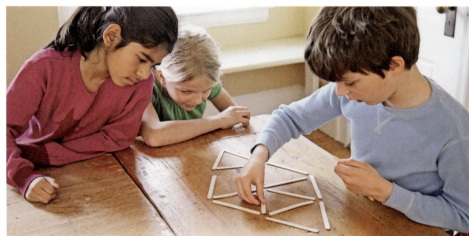

See pages 136–137 for solutions.

 1. Start with two small diamonds. Move four sticks to end up with one large diamond **(fig. 1)**.

2. Can you transform the spiral of sticks into two squares by moving three sticks **(fig. 2)**?

3. Remove three sticks to end up with four equal-size squares. Can you also figure out how to remove four sticks and end up with four equal-size squares **(fig. 3)**?

4. Move two sticks to end up with four equal-size squares **(fig. 4)**.

5. Start with a fish swimming to the right. Without moving the eye, can you move two sticks so that the fish is swimming straight up **(fig. 5)**?

6. Remove four sticks to end up with four equal-size triangles **(fig. 6)**.

FIG. 1

94 MATH LAB FOR KIDS

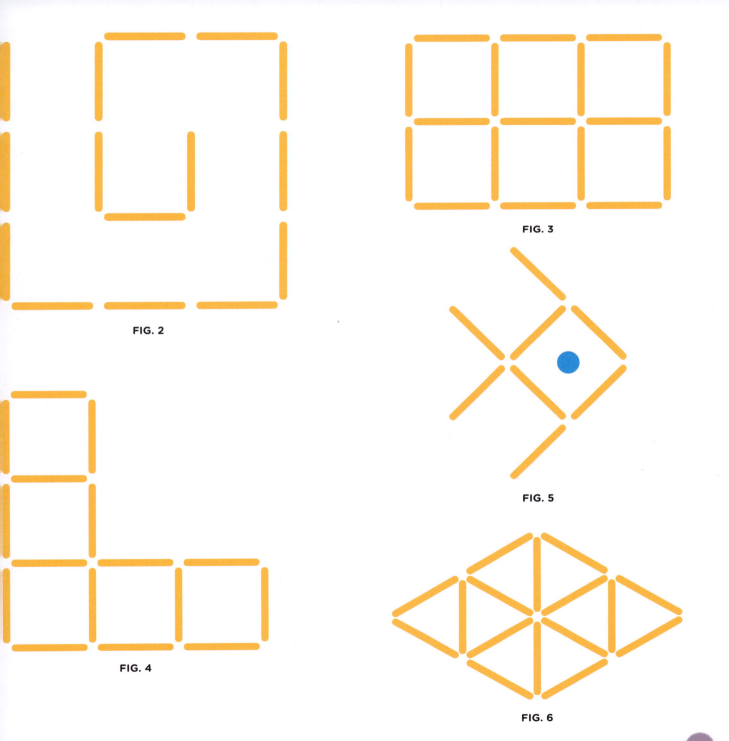

FIG. 2

FIG. 3

FIG. 5

FIG. 4

FIG. 6

TOOTHPICK PUZZLES

LAB 28
CHALLENGING TOOTHPICK PUZZLES

Materials

✔ Toothpicks, matchsticks, or craft sticks

✔ Pebble, bead, or penny for cup puzzle

MATH MEET
Invent Your Own Toothpick Puzzle

Stump your friends and family!

1. Make an arrangement of toothpicks.

2. Remov, add, or move toothpicks to make a second shape.

3. If you aren't happy with the possible puzzles from your starting arrangement, go back to step 1 and try again!

Puzzle makers try lots of configurations to invent puzzles. When you've found an arrangement you like, draw the starting placement for the sticks and write the instructions for the puzzle. On a separate paper, you might want to draw out the answer. Now you can share your puzzle with everyone!

Even more mind-bending puzzles! Start with your toothpicks as show in the figures. Then follow the instructions to transform the shapes.

PUZZLE PALOOZA

See page 137 for solutions.

1. This is two puzzles in one **(fig. 1)**.
- Move four sticks to get three equal squares.
- Move two sticks to make two rectangles.

2. Start with five squares **(fig. 2)**. Move two sticks so there are no squares left, but instead four identical shapes.

3. Move four sticks to create two arrows, each half the size of the starting arrow **(fig. 3)**.

4. Start with a ball inside a cup **(fig. 4)**. Move two sticks so that the ball is outside the cup. The cup should be the same size and shape—and don't move the ball!

96 MATH LAB FOR KIDS

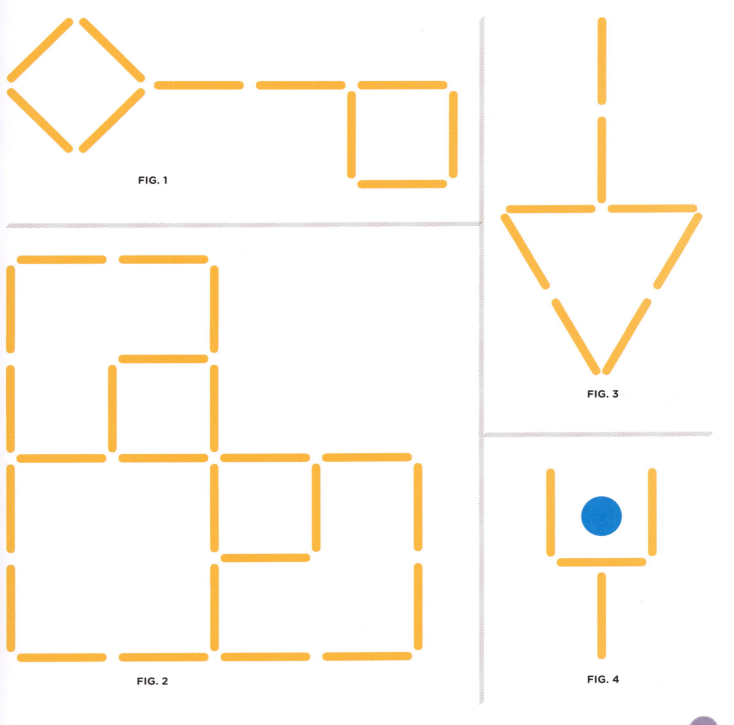

FIG. 1

FIG. 2

FIG. 3

FIG. 4

TOOTHPICK PUZZLES

8
THE GAME OF NIM

People believe that Nim is one of the oldest games invented. It was probably first played in China more than 1,000 years ago. Different versions of it are played all over the world. Do you think any games you like will still be played 1,000 years from now?

When you're playing a mathematical game with someone, you're not really trying to beat the other player. You're both working together to beat the game and figure out the winning strategies, so you should share your ideas with each other rather than keep them to yourself.

People sometimes ask how games can be math. There's a long history of mathematical games and an entire field of math called Game Theory. Games provide opportunities to test intuition, deepen mathematical understanding, and practice problem-solving strategies. Games allow mathematical ideas to emerge as players notice patterns, relationships, and winning strategies. And, of course, games are fun and provide a natural context for developing mathematical reasoning.

You should never lose Tic Tac Toe once you figure out the right strategy. If you don't already know the strategy, try to figure it out now. If you do already know how to never lose Tic Tac Toe, are there any other games you can think about like a mathematician?

LAB 29: LEARN TO PLAY NIM

Materials

✓ At least 20 similar objects (for example, pennies, blocks, toothpicks, beads, beans)

✓ Two players

In this lab, we learn how to play a game called Nim—and figure out how to win every time.

ACTIVITY 1: LEARN SIMPLE NIM

1. We'll start by learning a slightly simpler version of Nim.

- Player 1 makes a few groups of beads. She can make as many groups as she wants, but each group should have 1, 2, or 3 beads in it.

- Player 2 decides whether to play first or second.

- Players alternate turns. On each turn, the player must remove one or more beads from a single group. (The player is allowed to remove *all* the beads in a group.)

- Whoever takes the last bead wins.

2. Using these rules, play Nim with a partner at least five times to familiarize yourself with how it works. Before you begin, look at the practice game between Allanna and Zack **(figs. 1–6)**.

Parents are encouraged to play, too!

FIG. 1: Zack divides eight beads into three single-colored piles.

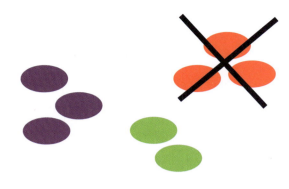

FIG. 2: Allanna decides to go first and takes all the red beads.

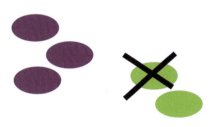

FIG. 3: Zack takes one green bead (leaving one in that pile).

FIG. 4: Allanna takes one purple bead (leaving two in that pile).

FIG. 5: Zack takes the last green bead.

FIG. 6: Allanna takes the last two purple beads and wins.

THE GAME OF NIM

LEARN TO PLAY NIM, *continued*

MATH TECHNIQUE
Try Simple Cases First

When working on a problem, mathematicians often tackle a simpler version of the problem first. Once they fully understand the simpler problem, they check to see if any strategies they used on the simpler problem apply to the harder problem they started with. In this chapter, we play simpler versions of Nim to develop strategies and see patterns. We'll learn the full rules at the end of the chapter.

ACTIVITY 2: Super-Simple Variations

VARIATION 1: PLAY FIVE GAMES USING JUST TWO GROUPS OF BEADS
In this variation, we modify the first rule on page 100 so that Player 1 can only make *two* piles of 1, 2, or 3 beads. Play this variation five times with your partner. See if you and your partner can discover any winning strategies.

VARIATION 2: PLAY THESE FIVE PRE-SET GAMES
Try the games set up below **(figs. 1–5)**. Play each game at least twice so that each player gets a chance to be Player 1 and Player 2. Can you figure out the winning strategy for each game? See page 138 for solutions.

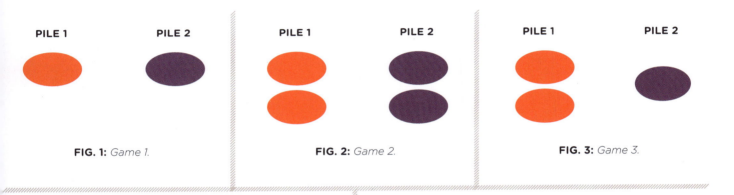

FIG. 1: *Game 1.*

FIG. 2: *Game 2.*

FIG. 3: *Game 3.*

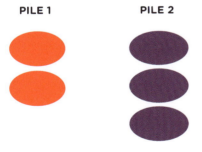

FIG. 4: *Game 4.*

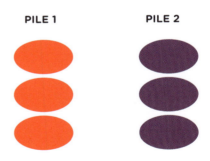

FIG. 5: *Game 5.*

THE GAME OF NIM

LAB 30
WIN NIM: THE COPYCAT STRATEGY

Materials

✔ At least 20 similar objects (for example, pennies, blocks, toothpicks, beads, beans)

✔ Two players

You may have noticed in the games with just two groups of beads that a winning strategy is to make sure the groups have the same number of beads in them. Then whenever your opponent makes a move, you can still make a move (the same one he or she just made).

COPYCAT STRATEGY

Calvin likes to annoy his opponent by copying her. Whenever he can, he makes the exact same move his opponent just made. For example, if Susie takes a group of two pieces away, Calvin will, too. A sample game between them is shown on the next page.

- Susie sets up the game and Calvin decides to go second **(figs. 1–4)**.
- If Susie had taken a pile with three beads on turn 1, Calvin would have too and he still would have won. Do you see why?
- Do you see how whatever Susie does, Calvin can copy her and win?
- Try playing a few more games of Nim using the copycat strategy.

MATH LAB FOR KIDS

FIG. 1: *On the first turn, Susie takes the pile with two green beads.*

FIG. 2: *On the second turn, Calvin takes the pile with two purple beads.*

FIG. 3: *On the third turn, Susie takes the pile with three red beads.*

FIG. 4: *On the fourth turn, Calvin takes the last pile and wins.*

THE GAME OF NIM

LAB 31
COPYCAT NIM AS PLAYER 1

Materials

✔ At least 20 similar objects (for example, pennies, blocks, toothpicks, beads, beans)

✔ Two players

Calvin's copycat strategy (see page 104) worked only because the piles were already even (two piles with two beads and two piles with three beads). But Calvin is so intent on being annoying by copying Susie that if he can't just copy Susie, he'll make a move so that next time he can copy her.

SETTING UP COPYCAT

Here's another way the copycat game could have gone:

1. Susie takes two yellow beads **(fig. 1)**.

2. Calvin takes two red beads **(fig. 2)**.

3. Susie takes the pile with two purple beads **(fig. 3)**.

4. Calvin takes the pile with two green beads **(fig. 4)**.

5. Susie takes the last red bead **(fig. 5)**.

6. Calvin takes the last yellow bead and wins **(fig. 6)**.

What if Susie had set up the game in **fig. 7** instead? Calvin would have chosen to go first and taken the new pile with one bead. Now he will always be able to copy Susie's moves and win.

Try playing a few more games of Nim using what you just learned.

106   MATH LAB FOR KIDS

FIG. 1: *Susie takes two yellow beads.*

FIG. 2: *Calvin takes two red beads.*

FIG. 3: *Susie takes the pile with two purple beads.*

FIG. 4: *Calvin takes the pile with two green beads.*

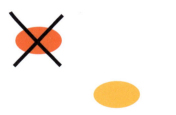

FIG. 5: *Susie takes the last red bead.*

FIG. 6: *Calvin takes the last yellow bead and wins.*

FIG. 7: *Another game for Susie and Calvin. If Calvin goes first and takes the blue bead, he can win by copying Susie.*

THE GAME OF NIM

LAB 32
WIN NIM: 1 + 2 = 3 STRATEGY

Materials

✔ At least 20 similar objects (for example, pennies, blocks, toothpicks, beads, beans)

✔ Two players

In Lab 30, we learned to use the copycat strategy. In Lab 31, we learned how to set up games so we can be copycats. Now we're two steps ahead. No matter what your opponent does, you can use the copycat strategy.

COPYCAT NIM: 1 + 2 = 3

Try the game in **fig. 1** with your partner. Calvin figured out a way to always win this one, too. Play it a few times with your partner and try to figure out Calvin's trick.

SOLUTIONS

1. The key is to get to a copycat game. Let your partner go first. If your partner takes the red pile, take one purple bead, then there will be two piles with one bead each and you'll win **(figs. 2–4)**.

2. If your partner takes the purple or green pile, take the same number from the red pile. Then the game will be even again **(figs. 5–7)**.

So a pile of three beads can always be balanced by a pile with one bead plus a pile with two beads. Pretty sneaky.

TRY THIS!
Full Nim Rules

In this chapter, we've been playing a slightly simplified version of Nim by saying that no pile can have more than three beads in it. In the original game, piles can be as large as you want. There are more tricks—like the one you just learned—waiting for you to discover if you try the full game.

108   MATH LAB FOR KIDS

FIG. 1: *A new setup for copycat Nim.*

FIG. 2: *Your partner takes the red pile.*

FIG. 3: *You take one purple bead.*

FIG. 4: *Two piles with one bead each means you'll win!*

FIG. 5: *Your partner takes the purple pile.*

FIG. 6: *You take the same amount of beads from the red pile.*

FIG. 7: *Both remaining piles are even.*

THE GAME OF NIM

GRAPH THEORY

Graph Theory is the study of how things are interconnected. This includes how computers are connected to each other in your house and on the Internet, how to efficiently place power plants to provide electricity in cities, the best locations to put fast food restaurants so that no one is too far from their favorite junk food, how to plan airplane flight paths, and more.

In 1736, mathematician Leonhard Euler solved the Bridges of Königsberg problem (see below), inventing Graph Theory in the process.

One of the most famous Graph Theory problems involves the city of Königsberg. Spanning both sides of a river, it has two islands, which are connected to the rest of the city by seven bridges. Citizens challenged each other to find a path that started and ended in the same place and crossed each of the seven bridges exactly once. Can you find such a path?

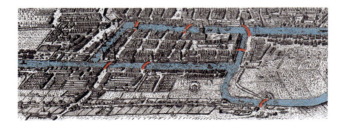

111

LAB 33: EULERIAN CIRCUITS

Materials

✔ Pencil
✔ Paper

You can avoid lifting your pencil by following the direction of the arrows when tracing the figure eight.

Learn how to trace shapes without lifting your pencil. To trace every line of the figure eight (left) without lifting your pencil, trace in the direction of the arrows as shown on the bottom.

TRACING EULERIAN CIRCUITS

The paths we draw in this lab *travel over every edge* of the entire graph, *start and end on the same vertex*, and *don't retrace any edges*. Mathematicians call these paths *Eulerian circuits*.

Important: Lines are allowed to cross but you can't trace over the same line twice.

1. Can you trace a five-point star without lifting your pencil or going over the same line twice **(fig. 1)**?

2. It's possible to trace all the shapes on the next page starting and ending at the same vertex without lifting your pencil or going over the same line twice **(figs. 2–6)**. Can you find the paths?

MATH FACT

In math, a *graph* is a set of dots, called *vertices*, connected by lines, called *edges*. You can also think of a *vertex* (the singular of vertices) as a corner. Note that edges don't have to be straight.

112 MATH LAB FOR KIDS

FIG. 1: *A five-point star.*

FIG. 2: *A simple house shape.*

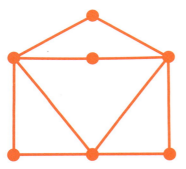
FIG. 3: *An open envelope.*

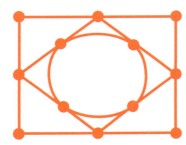
FIG. 4: *Nested shapes.*

FIG. 5: *A seven-point star.*

FIG. 6: *A seven-point star inside out.*

MEET THE MATHEMATICIAN FAN CHUNG

Fan Chung is an American mathematician who was born in Taiwan. She is a

Distinguished Professor of Mathematics and Computer Science at the University of California San Diego. Her main area of research is Graph Theory, including graphs of very large networks such as the Internet. In college, she met many female mathematicians. They all talked about math and helped each other, which encouraged her to become a mathematician. Fan says, "Frequently a good problem from someone else will give you a push in the right direction, and the next thing you know you have another good problem. You make mathematical friends and share the fun!"

The Power Grid Graph
Photo by Derrick Benzanson and Fan Chung

LAB 34: SECRETS OF EULERIAN CIRCUITS REVEALED

Materials

✔ Pencil
✔ Paper

What will you discover about the mathematically mysterious Eulerian circuits?

A SECRET SHORTCUT

In Lab 33, we discovered three rules for creating an Eulerian circuit:

1. Start and end from the same vertex.
2. Don't lift your pencil.
3. Don't retrace any edges.

In this lab, we'll learn a shortcut for figuring out if a graph has an Eulerian circuit.

1. You cannot follow the rules for creating an Eulerian circuit to draw this shape **(fig. 1)**. Try it and you'll see it's impossible.

2. What about **figs. 2–6**? Some of them have Eulerian circuits and others do not. Circle the ones that have an Eulerian circuit and put an "X" next to the ones that don't.

3. As we discovered, some graphs have no Eulerian circuit. Can you figure out a rule that will tell you if a shape has an Eulerian circuit?

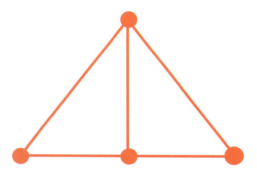

FIG. 1: *A triangle graph with no Eulerian circuit.*

114 MATH LAB FOR KIDS

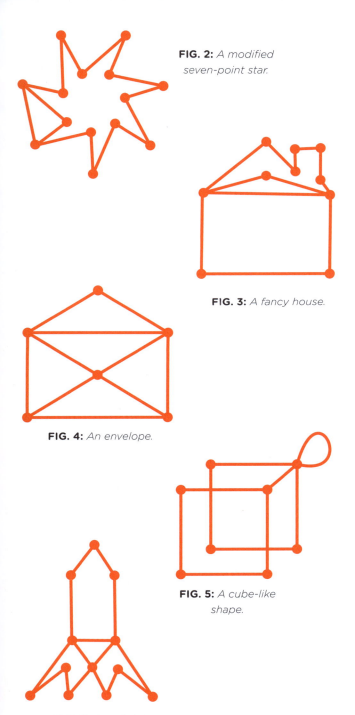

FIG. 2: *A modified seven-point star.*

FIG. 3: *A fancy house.*

FIG. 4: *An envelope.*

FIG. 5: *A cube-like shape.*

FIG. 6: *A rocket.*

What's Going On?

For every graph in Labs 33 and 34, write the number of edges coming out of each vertex next to the vertex. (*Hint*: Every graph in Lab 33 *does* have an Eulerian circuit.) For example:

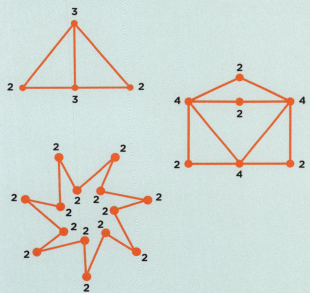

Do you see a pattern? Is there something that all the graphs with an Eulerian circuit have in common? Is there something that all the graphs without an Eulerian circuit have in common? Stop here and think about it.

Here's the answer: If there is an Eulerian circuit, then every time you go to a vertex, you leave it on a different edge until you get back to the beginning vertex. This means there must be an even number of edges (2, 4, 6, etc.) at every vertex. If any vertex connects an odd number of edges, you automatically know that the graph does *not* have an Eulerian circuit. An exciting discovery is that if every vertex in a graph has an even number of edges, the graph *does* have an Eulerian circuit.

GRAPH THEORY: MAKING CONNECTIONS

LAB 35 BRIDGES OF KÖNIGSBERG

Materials

✔ Map of Königsberg (see below)
✔ Pencil

Now that you know so much about Graph Theory, let's solve the Bridges of Königsberg problem from the Think About It on page 111.

GOING FROM MAP TO GRAPH

1. Turn the map below into a graph, as shown in **fig. 1**. Each area you can visit becomes a vertex of a graph. Each bridge between areas becomes an edge connecting those vertices.

2. The Bridges of Königsberg challenge is the same as finding an Eulerian circuit on the graph we just drew. Can you find an Eulerian circuit on this graph? If you get stuck, go on to the next step.

3. Hmm, maybe there isn't an Eulerian circuit. Let's label every vertex with the number of edges it connects **(fig. 2)**.

What's Going On?

Even if you can't find a path that crosses every bridge in Königsberg exactly once and ends up where you started, that doesn't mean no path exists! To solve the problem, we have to prove that there cannot be a path. We'll learn how to do a mathematical proof in this lab.

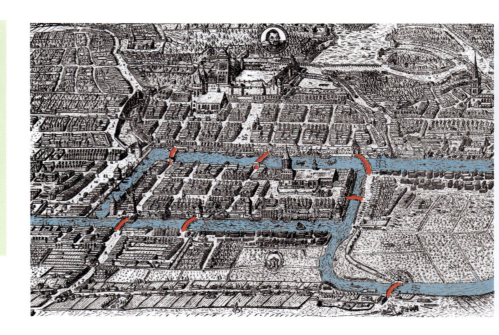

116 MATH LAB FOR KIDS

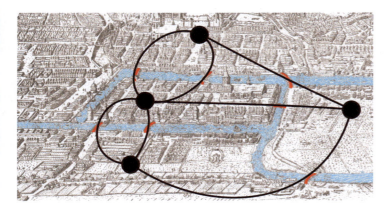

FIG. 1: *Turn the map into a graph.*

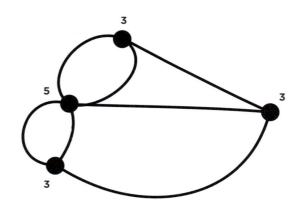

FIG. 2: *Label every vertex with the number of edges it connects.*

Now we know we weren't imagining it—there's no Eulerian circuit Remember, in Lab 34, we learned that if any vertex connects an odd number of edges, the graph does not have an Eulerian circuit. Here, *all* of the vertices connect an odd number of edges. Congratulations, you just did a proof by contradiction!

MATH TECHNIQUE
Proof by Contradiction

A mathematical *proof* is a series of logical arguments showing that something is true. There are many kinds of proofs. We explore two in this chapter (see Lab 36).

A *proof by contradiction* uses a series of arguments to show that if one thing is true, this means a second thing must be true. But here's the trick: If we can show that the second thing is actually false, that means that the first thing must have been false as well!

For example, for the Bridges of Königsberg problem, we know that if there is a path around the city, the graph will have an Eulerian circuit. We also know that if the graph has an Eulerian circuit, then all vertices must have an even number of edges coming out of it. But we showed that none of the vertices had an even number of edges! That means there cannot be a path that crosses every bridge exactly once and returns to where it started, so we've proven that a path cannot exist.

GRAPH THEORY: MAKING CONNECTIONS

LAB 36: THE EULER CHARACTERISTIC

Materials

- Pencil
- Paper

Learn an interesting relationship between vertices, edges, and regions.

COUNTING VERTICES, REGIONS, AND EDGES

Earlier, we said that a *graph* is a set of dots, called *vertices*, connected by lines, called *edges*. The paper you draw the graph on is divided into *regions*, each surrounded by edges. The space *outside the graph* also counts as a region. In the picture below, there are 10 vertices (colored black), 7 regions (colored yellow or green), and 15 edges (colored blue).

Leonhard Euler noticed something interesting about graphs when he counted

(number of vertices) + (number of regions) − (number of edges)

Let's count the number of vertices, edges, and regions in some graphs and see if we can figure out what he noticed.

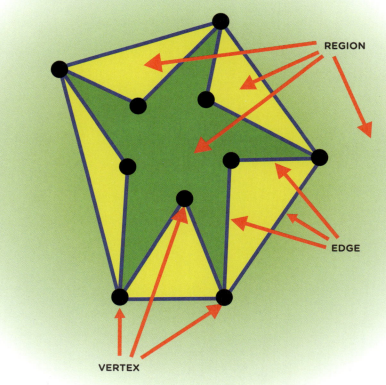

118 MATH LAB FOR KIDS

1. Figs. 1–3 show some examples where we've counted the vertices, edges, and regions of some graphs. You count them too and make sure your counts match ours! Remember to count the "outside" region.

Once we've counted V, R, and E, we'll add the number of vertices and regions together, subtract the number of edges, and see what we get!

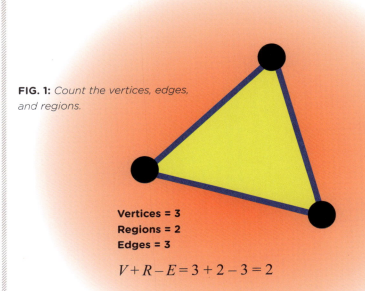

FIG. 1: *Count the vertices, edges, and regions.*

Vertices = 3
Regions = 2
Edges = 3

$$V + R - E = 3 + 2 - 3 = 2$$

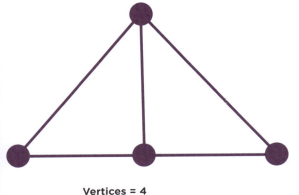

FIG. 2: *Remember to count the "outside" region.*

Vertices = 4
Regions = 3
Edges = 5

$$V + R - E = 4 + 3 - 5 = 2$$

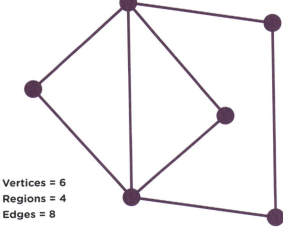

FIG. 3: *Do your counts match ours?*

Vertices = 6
Regions = 4
Edges = 8

$$V + R - E = 6 + 4 - 8 = 2$$

GRAPH THEORY: MAKING CONNECTIONS

THE EULER CHARACTERISTIC, *continued*

2. Now you try counting yourself **(figs. 4–10)**. Don't forget to count the "outside" region. How many vertices, edges, and regions do the following graphs have? Also calculate $V+R-E$ for each graph. *Hint:* The graphs in **figs. 9 and 10** only have one region: the "outside" region.

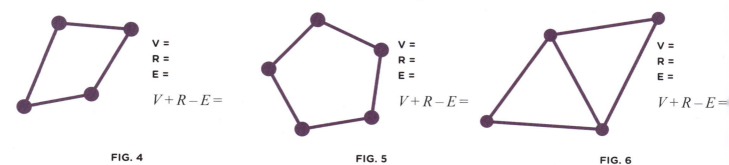

FIG. 4   FIG. 5   FIG. 6

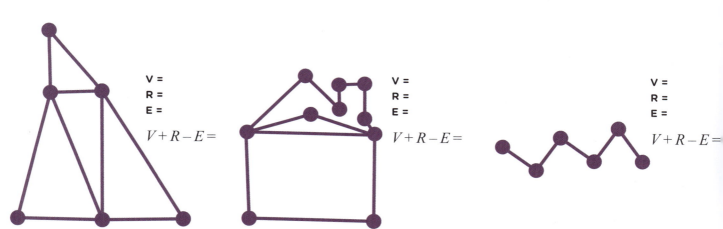

FIG. 7   FIG. 8   FIG. 9

FIG. 10

SOLUTION: In every example, $V+R-E=2$. That's pretty amazing. Do you think it's always true? (You might want to think about this for a bit before you continue on.)

120   MATH LAB FOR KIDS

Requirements for the Euler Characteristic to Be 2

Calculate the Euler Characteristic $(V + R - E)$ of this graph:

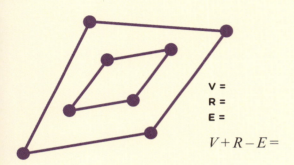

V =
R =
E =

$V + R - E =$

This graph is not *connected*. (Some vertices have no path between them.) We can connect it by adding an edge. Calculate the Euler Characteristic of the newly connected graph.

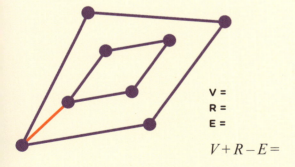

V =
R =
E =

$V + R - E =$

You got 2, right?

In the graph below, the two inside edges cross but there's no vertex where they cross. (Don't worry about why one edge is a different color quite yet.) What is the Euler Characteristic of this graph?

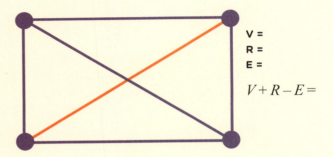

V =
R =
E =

$V + R - E =$

In Graph Theory, a *planar* graph has no crossing edges. (If there is a vertex where two edges meet, that's not considered crossing edges and it's still a planar graph.) Let's move the red edge outside as below so the graph becomes planar. What is the Euler Characteristic of the newly planar graph?

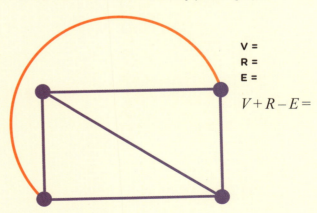

V =
R =
E =

$V + R - E =$

Now Euler's characteristic is 2 again!

GRAPH THEORY: MAKING CONNECTIONS

LAB 37: A PROOF ABOUT THE EULER CHARACTERISTIC

Materials

- ✔ Pencil
- ✔ Paper

In a **PROOF BY INDUCTION,** *you first show that the simplest case (called the* **BASE CASE***) is true. Next you prove the* **INDUCTION STEP,** *showing that a general case being true means that the following case is also true. Now you have a recipe showing how to get from any size to any other size (repeating the induction step as many times as needed, even going on forever), so you know it's always true. (This is college-level math, so don't worry if you find it a bit confusing.) Let's show that the Euler Characteristic is 2 for all planar, connected graphs!*

CHALLENGE!: PROOF BY INDUCTION

1. Base case: Calculate $V + R - E$ in the case of a single vertex and no edges **(fig. 1)**. It's 2, right?

2. Calculate $V + R - E$ when we add a new edge and a new vertex **(fig. 2)**. It's still 2. We added one new vertex and one new edge, so they canceled each other out.

3. Calculate $V + R - E$ before and after we add a new edge but not a new vertex **(figs. 3-4)**. It's still 2, because when we add a new edge but no new vertex, we end up adding a new region, which cancels out the new edge. Try adding one edge to some of the graphs from earlier in this chapter. Do you see how we always add one region when we add one edge? Thus, $V + R - E$ stays the same.

4. We can build any planar connected graph by adding vertices and/or edges as in the steps above. Try adding edges and/or vertices to the graphs in **figs. 5-7**. Calculate $V + R - E$ before and after.

5. Add some vertices and/or edges to a few graphs you make up yourself. Calculate $V + R - E$ before and after. You can try this on *any* planar connected graph, not just the simple ones from steps 1 and 2.

If you add just an edge, that ends up adding a new region. If you add a new vertex, you have to add the edge to connect it to the existing graph. Thus, at every step of building a planar connected graph, $V + R - E = 2$. Amazing!

You have just done a mathematical proof by induction. Congratulations!

FIG. 1: Calculate $V + R - E$ in the case of a single vertex and no edges.

FIG. 2: Calculate $V + R - E$ when we add a new edge and a new vertex.

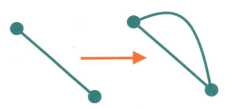

FIG. 3: Calculate $V + R - E$ before and after we add a new edge.

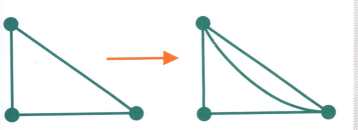

FIG. 4: Calculate $V + R - E$ before and after we add a new edge.

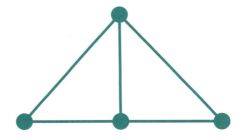

FIG. 5: Calculate $V + R - E$ before and after adding vertices and edges.

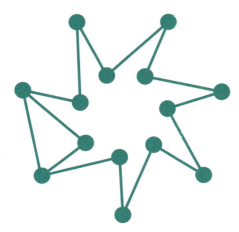

FIG. 6: Calculate $V + R - E$ before and after adding vertices and edges.

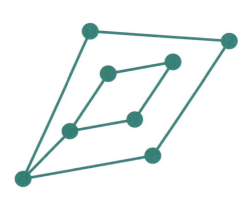

FIG. 7: Calculate $V + R - E$ before and after adding vertices and edges.

GRAPH THEORY: MAKING CONNECTIONS

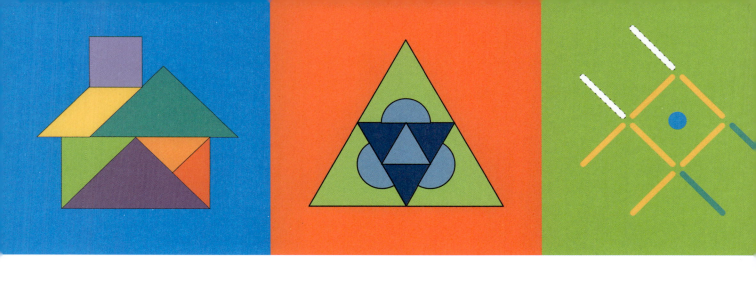

PULL-OUTS

SOUTH AMERICA MAP

See Lab 12, page 46.

PULL-OUTS 125

AFRICA MAP *See Lab 13, page 50.*

EQUILATERAL TRIANGLE TEMPLATE

See Labs 18–20, pages 68–77.

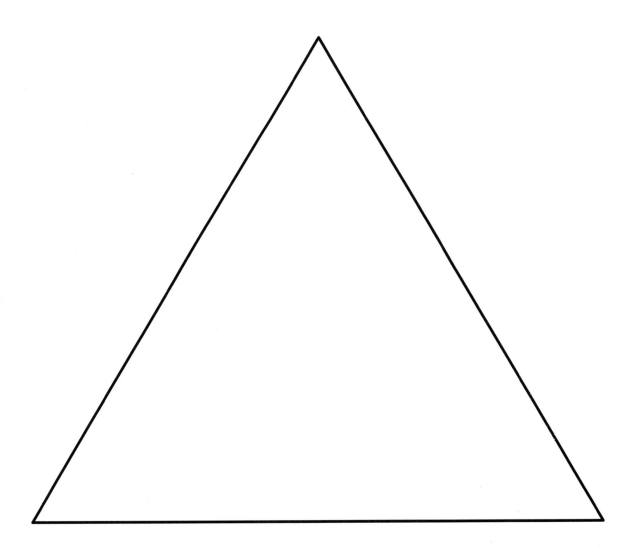

PULL-OUTS

TANGRAMS

See Labs 23–25, pages 84–89.

PULL-OUTS 129

HINTS AND SOLUTIONS

1. GEOMETRY: LEARN ABOUT SHAPES

Think About It: There are lots of ways to make a 3D shape from a triangle. A triangular prism is like a really thick triangle, and if you look at it from above it looks like a triangle. A pyramid takes a shape and raises it up in a point, so that if you look at it from the side it looks like a triangle. There are lots of 3D shapes with triangle faces.

LAB 1, Try this!:

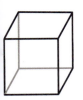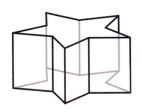

Prisms starting from a four-sided shape, a five-sided shape, and a star.

LAB 2, Try this!:

A pyramid starting from a star-shaped base. Shapes that you cannot turn into a pyramid include a circle, figure eight, and more you might think of.

LAB 3

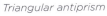

Triangular antiprism

Pentagonal antiprism

LAB 4, Octahedron: Some ways in which the octahedron is different from the tetrahedron: Octahedron: 8 sides, 6 vertices, 12 edges. Tetrahedron: 4 sides, 4 vertices, 6 edges. Every corner of the octahedron connects to four triangles. Every corner of the tetrahedron connects to three triangles.

Compare the octahedron you built to the triangular antiprism that you built in Lab 3, step 6. What do you notice? They're the same shape!

2. TOPOLOGY: MIND-BENDING SHAPES

LAB 9

- **Activity 1, step 4:** Yes, you can make a triangle and many other shapes.
- **Activity 2:** You can stretch or squeeze the bag to make it look like a ball, cube, or bowl, but not like a doughnut or mug.
- **Scavenger Hunt** *hint*: Here are some examples of objects in each category to get you started.
  1. No holes: book, plate, cup (no handles)
  2. One hole: cup with handle, CD, bead
  3. Two holes: unzipped coat, grocery bag (if it has two handles)
  4. More than two holes: sieve, slatted chair, sweater

LAB 10

- **Activity 1, step 7:** The Möbius strip has one edge.
- **Activity 2, step 1:** You end up with two crowns.

- **Activity 2, step 2:** You end up with a single long band that has two full twists.

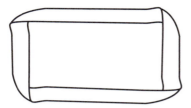

- **Activity 3, step 2:** If you draw a line on the crown, the other side of the crown (inside) is blank. For the Möbius strip, there are no blank places. (There is only one side.)
- **Activity 3, step 3:** You end up with three crowns.
- **Activity 3, step 4:**

You end up with a long band with multiple twists interlinked with a small Möbius strip.

Try this!:
You should get these results.

How Many Sides?	One	Two
Zero twists		✓
One half twist	✓	
Two half twist		✓
Three half twist	✓	
Four half twist		✓

LAB 11

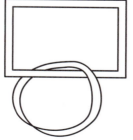

This is the shape you will get when you cut. Surprised?

3. COLORING MAPS LIKE A MATHEMATICIAN

LAB 12
Step 2: There are multiple possible solutions, but you shouldn't need more than three colors.

Step 3: There are multiple possible solutions, but you shouldn't need more than two colors for Triangle Map 1 and three colors for Triangle Map 2.

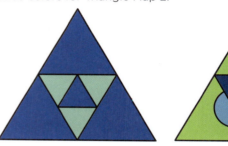

Step 4: There are multiple possible solutions, but you shouldn't need more than two colors for the Seven-Point Star Map and three colors for Modified Seven-Point Star Map.

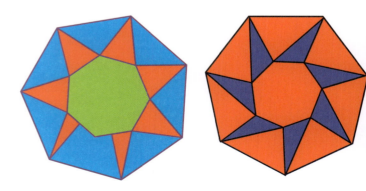

132 MATH LAB FOR KIDS

LAB 12, Try this!:
South America Map: Paraguay's neighbors surround it and also touch each other such that four colors are needed for those four countries.

LAB 13
There are multiple possible solutions, but you shouldn't need more than four colors for the Bird, Africa, and Abstract Maps.

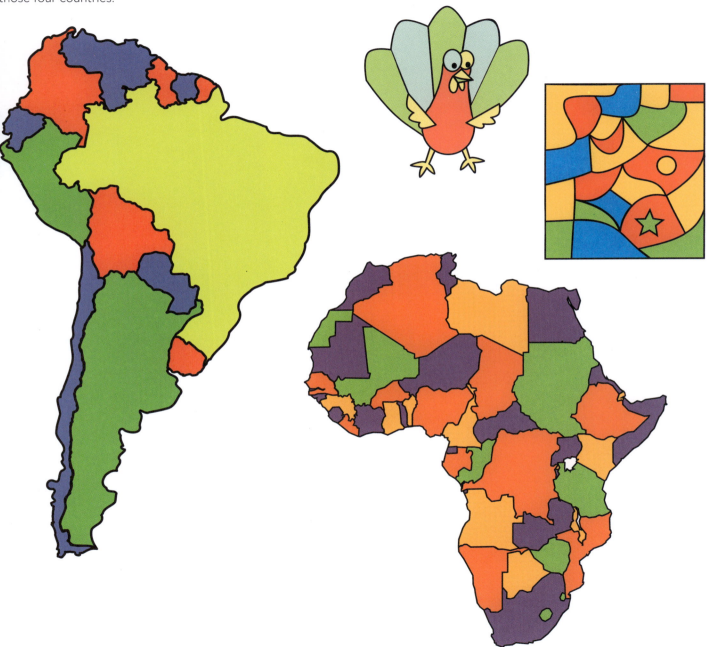

HINTS AND SOLUTIONS   133

5. FANTASTIC FRACTALS

LAB 19, Try this!:
- The perimeter of a Sierpinski triangle is infinite. Every time we add more (smaller) triangles to a Sierpinski triangle, the perimeter gets 1.5 times larger than the previous iteration.
- Every time you do an iteration of the Sierpinski triangle, you get 3 times more triangles. (Every triangle in the previous iteration gets divided into three.) So the pattern goes 1, 3, 9, 27, etc. In the full Sierpinski, after infinite iterations, there are an infinite number of triangles.

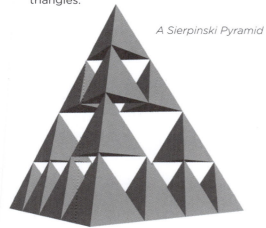

A Sierpinski Pyramid

LAB 21, Try this!:

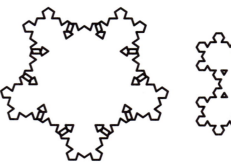

Pentagon and hexagon examples.

LAB 22, Try this!:
Notice that no matter how many smaller triangles we add to the sides of a Koch snowflake, the entire shape never extends very far. So we know the area is somewhat less than the circle we've drawn. (The exact answer for the area of a Koch snowflake with infinitely many triangles added is 8/5 times the area of the original triangle.) Even if you can't get an exact answer, being able to get an upper bound (it has to be less than the size of the circle) is a really interesting result.

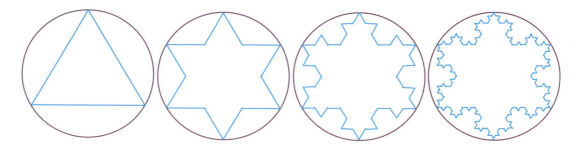

6. TERRIFIC TANGRAMS

LAB 23

Think About It:

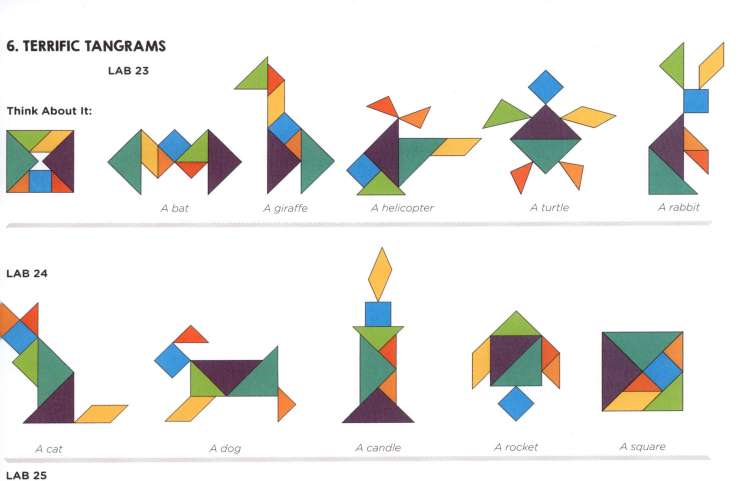

LAB 24

LAB 25

HINTS AND SOLUTIONS   135

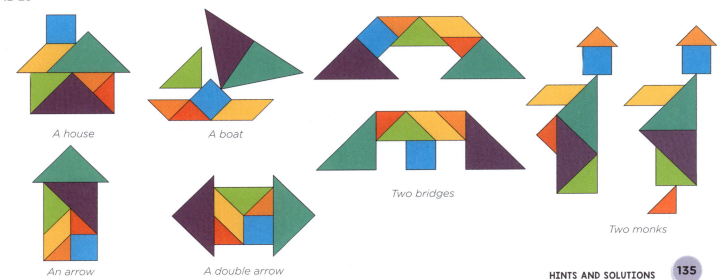

7. TOOTHPICK PUZZLES

Think About It: There are 16 triangles in the image.

LAB 26, Activity 2:

LAB 27

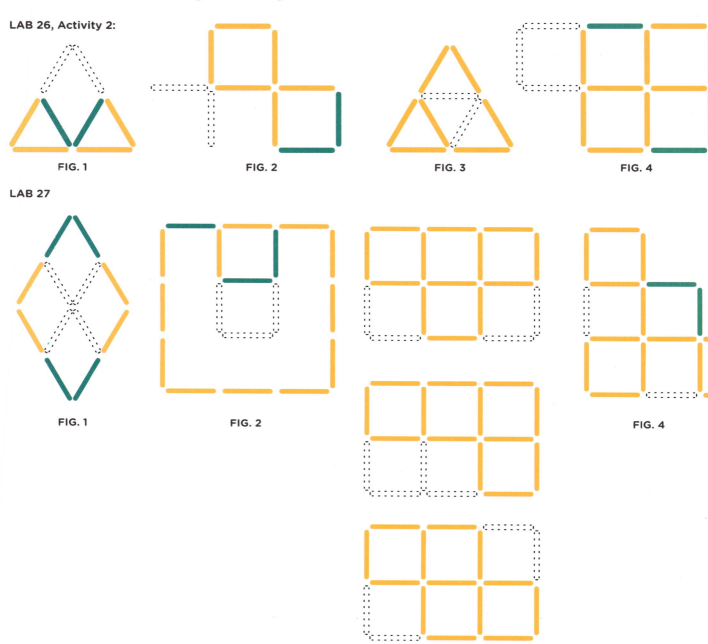

LAB 27, continued:

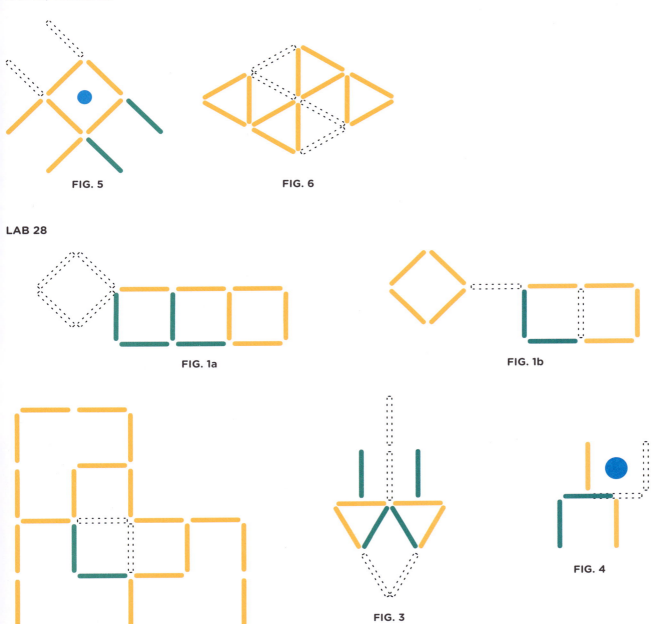

FIG. 5

FIG. 6

LAB 28

FIG. 1a

FIG. 1b

FIG. 2

FIG. 3

FIG. 4

HINTS AND SOLUTIONS

8. THE GAME OF NIM

LAB 29, Activity 2, Variation 2

Game 1:

    Player 2 always wins.

Game 2:

Player 2 can always win if he or she plays as follows:
- If Player 1 takes one bead, Player 2 should take one bead from the *other pile*. Then no matter what Player 1 does on turn three, Player 2 will win on turn four.

  OR

- If Player 1 takes two beads (a whole pile), Player 2 can take the whole other pile and win.

Game 3:

If Player 1 takes either whole pile, Player 2 can take the other whole pile and win. BUT if Player 1 takes one bead from the first pile, then Player 2 takes one bead from either pile on turn two (both only have one bead) and Player 1 wins on turn three. So Player 1 has a move that makes Player 1 always win, whereas Player 2 can only win if Player 1 makes a mistake.

Game 4:

- If Player 1 takes all of pile 1 or 2, Player 2 can win by taking all of the other pile.
- If Player 1 takes one red bead, Player 2 can take two purple beads and then we have the same set-up as in Game 1, where Player 2 always wins.
- If Player 1 takes one purple bead, then he or she has reduced Game 4 to be the same as Game 2 and Player 1 can always win. (See Game 2.)

So Player 1 has a move (see last option above) that makes Player 1 always win, whereas Player 2 can only win if Player 1 makes a mistake.

Game 5:

Player 2 always wins (unless he or she makes a mistake).
- If Player 1 takes all of either pile, Player 2 takes all of the other pile and wins.
- If Player 1 takes one bead from either pile, the game is reduced to Game 4 and Player 2 has a move where he or she can always win.
- If Player 1 takes two beads from either pile, Player 2 can take two from the other pile and the game is reduced to Game 1, where Player 2 always wins.

9. GRAPH THEORY: MAKING CONNECTIONS

LAB 33: Follow the numbers in order to make the path.

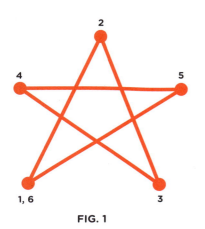

FIG. 1

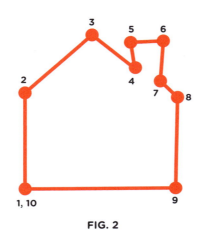

FIG. 2

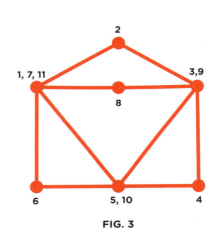

FIG. 3

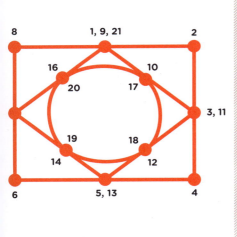

FIG. 4

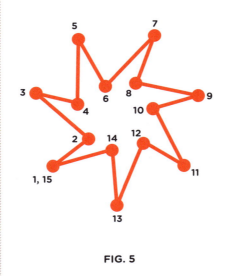

FIG. 5

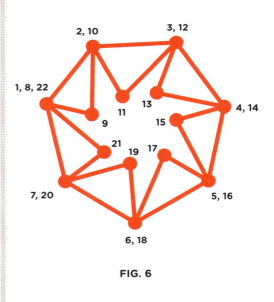

FIG. 6

HINTS AND SOLUTIONS 139

LAB 34: These two graphs have Eulerian circuits.

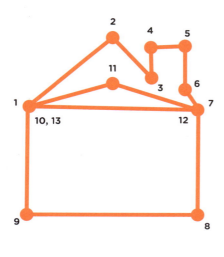

FIG. 3

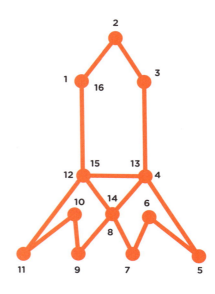

FIG. 6

LAB 35, step 3: We can tell that there is no Eulerian circuit because in Lab 34 we discovered that there must be an even number of edges coming out of each vertex in order to have an Eulerian circuit.

LAB 36, step 2:

V = 4
R = 2
E = 4

$V + R - E = 4 + 2 - 4 = 2$

FIG. 4

V = 5
R = 2
E = 5

$V + R - E = 5 + 2 - 5 = 2$

FIG. 5

V = 4
R = 3
E = 5

$V + R - E = 4 + 3 - 5 = 2$

FIG. 6

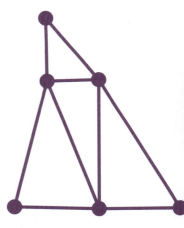

V = 6
R = 5
E = 9

$V + R - E = 6 + 5 - 9 = 2$

FIG. 7

LAB 36, step 2, continued:

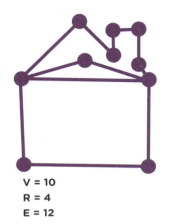

V = 10
R = 4
E = 12

$V + R - E = 10 + 4 - 12 = 2$

FIG. 8

V = 6
R = 1
E = 5

$V + R - E = 6 + 1 - 5 = 2$

FIG. 9

V = 6
R = 1
E = 5

$V + R - E = 6 + 1 - 5 = 2$

FIG. 10

Sidebar: Requirements for the Euler Characteristic to Be 2

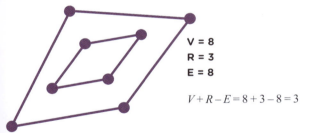

V = 8
R = 3
E = 8

$V + R - E = 8 + 3 - 8 = 3$

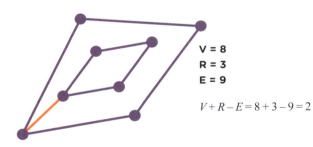

V = 8
R = 3
E = 9

$V + R - E = 8 + 3 - 9 = 2$

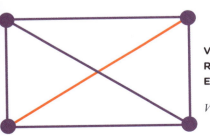

V = 4
R = 5
E = 6

$V + R - E = 4 + 5 - 6 = 3$

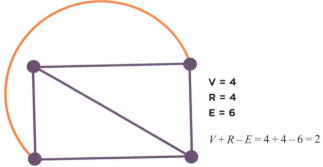

V = 4
R = 4
E = 6

$V + R - E = 4 + 4 - 6 = 2$

HINTS AND SOLUTIONS

ACKNOWLEDGMENTS

Rebecca would like to thank her parents, Ron and Joan, for teaching her to write clearly, concisely, and grammatically correctly. And a second round of thanks to her father for making her think writing a book is a normal thing to do.

She would also like to thank her husband, Dean, for his support throughout the process.

Rebecca's fabulous eldest child, Allanna, caused her to realize this book needed to be written. Allanna and her brother, the forever inquisitive Zack, were not only enthusiastic about the idea of Mom writing a book but also cheerfully play-tested some of the book's content. Rebecca looks forward to working through all the labs with her youngest, Xander, when he's old enough. In the meantime, she appreciates the good humor and joy all three bring into her life every day.

We would both like to acknowledge how much fun it was to work on this book together. It was a great collaborative effort and resulted in something we're both proud of. The book also gave us a wonderful opportunity to continue the meaningful work we began at the STEAM (science, technology, engineering, art, and math) after-school enrichment center we helped build.

J.A. would like to thank Rebecca for her patience, her enthusiasm, and for the opportunity for this collaboration that taught each of us some new things and strengthened our long-time friendship. This was a wonderful chance to improve my own ideas by bouncing them off someone I trust, learn a bunch of really cool new stuff (whether it made it into the book or not!), and share many truly terrible math jokes.

We owe a big debt of gratitude to all the people who helped us test and hone the book's content, especially the staff and students of Birches School in Lincoln, Massachusetts, whose cheerful faces brighten up this book's pages.

J.A.'s math professor mother, Kathie, provided valuable feedback on the book's content and her enthusiasm in working every lab made us happy.

Of course, we'd like to thank our editor, Joy, and Tiffany for pitching the book idea to us and Quarry in the first place. Meredith and Anne were invaluable in making this book look as good as it does.

Finally, we'd like to thank all the staff at Quarry Books who worked on this book for helping us put such a beautiful, full-color romp through math out into the world.

ABOUT THE AUTHORS

Rebecca Rapoport holds degrees in mathematics from Harvard and Michigan State. From her first job out of college, as one of the pioneers of Harvard's Internet education offerings, she has been passionate about encouraging her love of math in others.

As an early contributor to both retail giant Amazon.com and Akamai Technologies, the No. 1 firm in cloud computing, Rapoport played a key role in several elements of the Internet revolution.

Rapoport returned to her first love, education, as an innovator of new methods to introduce children and adults to the critically important world of STEM as COO of Einstein's Workshop, an enrichment center dedicated to helping kids explore the creative side of science, technology, engineering, art, and math. One of their classes for six- to ten-year-olds is Recreational Math, which inspired the creation of this book.

Currently, Rapoport is developing and teaching innovative math curricula at Boston-area schools.

J.A. Yoder holds a degree in computer science from Caltech. She is an educator and engineer who has a lifetime love of puzzles and patterns. Her educational philosophy is that hands-on creative work is both the most fun and the most effective way to learn. She developed and taught the original hands-on-math lessons for an after-school program that eventually inspired this book. Some of her happiest memories come from "eureka moments"—either from learning something that makes a dozen other things suddenly make sense, or the sense of accomplishment that comes from solving a clever puzzle. The only thing better is sharing this joy with others.

RESOURCES

Go to **mathlabforkids.com** or **quartoknows.com/page/math-lab** for printable versions of some exercises and pull-out pages in this book.

National Council of Teachers of Mathematics
There is some great material in the "Classroom Resources" section. www.nctm.org

Fractal Foundation
Check out the Fractivities and other content in the Explore Fractals section. http://fractalfoundation.org

Zome
Geometric building toy. http://zometool.com

THANK YOU!

INDEX

A
Antiprisms, 16–17

B
Boole, Mary Everest, 64
Bridges of Königsberg, 111, 116–117

C
Circles
    about, 24
    making, 24–25, 30–31
    transforming, 36
Creative curves, 64–65
Cubes, 18, 19
Curve stitching
    about, 57
    creative curves, 64–65
    parabolas, 58–61
    stars, 62–63

D
Dodecahedron, 18, 21–22

E
Ellipses, 28–29, 32–33
Equilateral triangles
    about, 26
    template, 127
Euler, Leonhard, 111
Eulerian circuits
    Euler characteristic, 118–121
    Euler proof, 122–123
    secret shortcut, 114–115
    tracing, 112–113

F
Fan Chung, 113
Four Color Theorem, 45
Fractals
    about, 67
    hints and solutions, 134
    Koch snowflakes, 74–77, 80–81
    Sierpinski triangles, 69–73
    square snowflakes, 78–79

G
Geometry
    about, 11
    antiprisms, 16–17
    circles, 24–25, 30–31, 36
    ellipses, 28–29, 32–33
    hints and solutions, 131
    Platonic solids, 18–23
    prisms, 12–13
    pyramids, 14–15
    triangles, 26–27, 127
Graph Theory
    about, 111
    Bridges of Königsberg problem, 111, 116–117
    Eulerian circuits, 112–115
        Euler characteristic, 118–121
        Euler proof, 122–123
    hints and solutions, 139–141
Graphs, about, 112, 118
Greedy Algorithm, 50

I
Icosahedrons, 18, 23

K
Koch snowflakes, 74–77, 80–81

M
Maps, coloring
    basics, 46–48
    efficiently, 50–52
    hints and solutions, 132–133
    planning, 49, 53
    squiggle, 54–55
    templates, 125–126
Möbius strips
    about, 38
    making crown and, 38–41
    making Möbius surprise, 42–43

N
Nim
    about, 99, 108
    copycat strategy, 104–107
    hints and solutions, 138
    learning to play, 100–101
    1+2=3 strategy, 108–109
    simple versions, 102–103
Numerical Analysis, 57

O
Octahedrons, 18, 20

P
Parabolas
    about, 58
    graphing, 58–61
    making stars with, 62–63
Platonic solids
    about, 18
    cubes, 19
    dodecahedron, 21–22
    icosahedrons, 23
    octahedrons, 20
    tetrahedrons, 18
Prisms, 12–13
Proof by contradiction, 117
Puzzles, using trial and error to solve, 93
    See also Tanagrams; Toothpick puzzles
Pyramids, 14–15

S
Sierpinski triangles
    area of, 72
    building, 70–71, 73
    drawing, 68–69
Snowflakes
    Koch, 74–77, 80–81
    square, 78–79
Stars, stitching, 62–63

T
Tangrams
    about, 83
    basics, 84–85
    hints and solutions, 135
    level two, 86
    level three, 88–89
    making own, 87
    rules, 84
    template, 129
Tetrahedrons, 18
Toothpick puzzles
    about, 91
    basic, 92–93
    hints and solutions, 136–137
    level two, 94–95
    level three, 96–97
    making own, 96
Topology
    about, 35, 37
    hints and solutions, 131–132
    Möbius strips, 38–43
    transformations, 36–37
Triangles, 26–27, 68–73, 127
Triangular prisms, making, 12–13

V
Vertices, defined, 112

W
Website, 9

144   MATH LAB FOR KIDS